Communion
Encounters

A Time of Awakening

Jay Brinegar

i

Cover design by Clara Rose

Literary consulting, editing, and formatting, by Clara Rose & Company.

Published by RoseDale Publishing
12100 Cobble Stone Drive, Suite 3
Bayonet Point, Florida 34667

ISBN- 979-8-9889895-9-2

Dedication

I want to dedicate this book to all the prayer warriors who continually seek God's face on our behalf and for the work God has called us to do. I also want to dedicate this to those who hunger for more of God's presence and glory in the body of Christ, and to all the church leaders seeking God for a new awakening that will brings millions to Christ around the world.

I dedicate this book to those in the fivefold ministry who God is raising up in this hour with special anointings and grace. I am especially thankful for my wife, Patti. Her love and support keep me going. The Bible says when a man finds a wife, he finds a good thing and obtains favor from the Lord. Indeed, she is a sign of God's favor in my life.

Most of all, I dedicate this book and its work to Jesus Christ who is my Lord and Savior.

Contents

Acknowledgment

I want to give a very sincere thank you to all of my friends and prayer partners who have diligently prayed over this book and for me throughout its creation. They have personally experienced the power of Communion and what I have shared in this work. Let us continue to cover Communion Encounters and the body of Christ in prayer and move forward together in this most opportune time.

Introduction

This is not just another book on Communion. It carries a prophetic message throughout its words and revelation that will bring a reformation in hearts and churches around the Lord's Table, the Holy Sacraments, which we also call Communion. It will bring revelation of Communion's role in past, present, and future awakenings. It has already begun.

This book will unveil the profound power of Communion, a power that will not only transform your personal life but also the life of the church. It will lead you to a deeper intimacy with the Lord and help you appropriate the blessings of the Covenant through the body and blood of Jesus.

Throughout the church, Communion is referenced by many names, such as The Lord's Supper, The Lord's Table, Breaking Bread, The Last Super, Holy Sacraments, Holy Communion, Communion, and Eucharist, to name a few. They all bring us to the Body and the Blood of Jesus, which is our focus. Throughout the book, I will use these terms interchangeably to make certain emphasis as I deem necessary. I mean no disrespect to the other references or how others may use them.

In late 2021, the Lord began to lead me on a journey

that would be life changing. He brought me into a deeper prayer life I had never experienced before, bringing me to a place of brokenness yet overwhelmed by His glorious presence.

My mornings started around four in the morning, praying on the floor of my study with my Bible and journal and having Communion. This personal journey with the Lord is one that many of you may relate to, and it is this connection that forms the heart of this book.

During that time, He led me to study specific past revivals and awakenings and showed me various overlays of repetition in each one. Much prayer, a burden for the lost, a need for repentance, and a heart cry for God's presence. These revivals were not neat and orderly but messy. Learning from the past will prepare us for the challenges that come with revival and awakening.

In May 2022, God started putting Indiana and Kentucky on my heart, and I regularly prayed over both states, the church leaders, and God's people. In the next four months, I became fascinated with the Holy Sacraments' powerful role in these awakenings and how they are still impacting us today.

Historical records, journals of ministers, and eyewitness accounts include undeniable facts, and each one became addictive reading. Communion gatherings of all sizes were the place God desired to bring revival and awakening. From tiny churches in the wilderness to thousands gathering in fields, God brought His glory and power.

In September 2022, God took me on a three-week journey through both states to pray. I did not preach in any churches, but I had multiple long meetings with several pastors I had never met before. In each meeting, the presence of God was overwhelming as I shared my vision with them. We all continued to pray in the weeks' ahead, knowing God was leading us into something special.

While I went to many places in both states, He specifically took me to Grand Rivers, Owensboro, Cain Ridge, and finally to Red River in Kentucky, where I spent many hours letting Him speak to my heart. I am not permitted to share those details yet.

In early prayer on November 22, 2022, the Lord told me that He had already started a revival and spiritual awakening in Indiana and Kentucky and was about to move it forward and accelerate it. I was to come alongside the pastors and churches to assist them in a particular way. I shared this directive with several of my ministry friends, and all bore witness to the fact that God was doing something special, and we must continue to pray, be watchful, and prepare.

Communion Encounters

On November 23, 2022, @ 4:00 am, the Holy Spirit gave me the Vision for Communion Encounters, and His glorious presence overwhelmed me. He told me to write the vision, and it was three pages long when it was finished.

In the early morning prayer on Dec 2, 2022, the Holy Spirit told me, *"Focus on the Communion Encounters – anywhere and everywhere. Revival and awakening are both birthed and maintained through them."* Again, He says, *"Do these and reach the communities. My people will gather."*

At that time, He provided more specific guidance concerning the Communion Encounter services and gave me a message for the body of Christ. This book is part of the message. When we come together to share in the Sacraments of Holy Communion, we will find ourselves hosting His presence as one in Him.

"Communion Encounters – Hosting The Presence Of God As One!"

Then, the Lord really got my attention. On February 8, 2023, a revival exploded at Asbury University in Wilmore, Kentucky, which lasted 16 days. It reached around the world, and 50,000 to 70,000 people attended. Many universities across America broke out in revivals as a result, and there is no way to grasp its worldwide impact today. The Lord had told me he was about to accelerate the revival and awakening, and He did. It was a confirmation He was leading us into something special.

Throughout this process, I've always had Communion during my prayer times. The experiential knowledge and understanding I gained while having Communion became very relevant when He led me to author this book. I tell you, get used to different. It will be much better!

We Are In A Kairos Moment

The Greek word Kairos, usually translated as time or opportunity, refers to a special occasion set in its proper time or season. Thayer defines it as a measure of time, a fixed and definite time, an opportune time or a seasonable time, a divinely appointed time with a beginning and an ending.

Many past revivals and awakenings happened in God-given Kairos moments, and the Scriptures are full of examples. Each one was uniquely special for its specific time, and the people responded to the open window of God and pressed in with prayer and repentance.

Do we not see this happening today?

Communion Encounters

I believe we are at a specific time in history with a particular window of opportunity that demands our response regarding Communion. We have been given a window that, if we embrace it, will significantly impact the church and the community through the salvation of many. It is a time of reformation on how we have Communion in the local church and the need to increase Communion in our personal lives.

It is a time for believers to come together in a Communion Encounter gathering to set our hearts as one in Jesus Christ as the center of it all. It is not about our ministries or churches. It is not about self-promotion and playing religious politics and positioning. It is about Jesus Christ and seeing Him Glorified. We are in a Kairos moment, and God's grace is upon it.

As I've taught various lessons on the bread and cups in this book and shared the vision of Communion Encounters in multiple churches and states, I've witnessed the incredible power of Communion transforming lives and ministries. People have been freed from addictions, oppression, and depression. Wounded and broken hearts have been healed, and many physical healings and miracles have occurred during Communion.

Pastors who attended the Communion Encounter

services gave tremendous and powerful testimonies of how they were personally changed by the more profound teaching and the way we shared in the body and blood of Jesus. They returned to their Churches, taught their congregations what they had learned, and then changed how they conducted Communion in their services. It was no longer just a check box in a program. The testimonies from pastors and members are truly inspiring.

These pastors recognized the need to expand a Christ-centered Communion and move away from the ten-minute ritual to experience the fullness of the covenant in Communion. They removed the time limitations and allowed the Holy Spirit to work in people's hearts. They let the Holy Spirit bring the required reformation into the hearts of God's people, church leaders, and their congregations and learned the power of multiple Communions in a service.

The Lord has been calling His people to pray and pray more, personally, and corporately. There is a great emphasis on seeking His presence, His face, and His glory, and the results in many churches and lives have been tremendous. The more we incorporate Communion, the more of His presence, power, and glory we experience and carry in our daily lives.

God is calling His people to a greater understanding

and participation in Communion. However, the experience is not gained by just reading about it in another book but by *actions in faith* based upon a process of active participation in the body and blood of Jesus, known as Communion.

I am confident that you're about to discover new and powerful revelations that will significantly impact your life. Welcome to Communion Encounters – A Time Of Awakening!

Chapter 1

Communion In The Awakened Church

Communion, one of three ordinances of Christianity, has been an integral part of the church since the day of Pentecost. It has been a vital part of many revivals and awakenings throughout the world.

Next to the day of Pentecost, there may not be a more historically significant Communion event than the Second Great Awakening, which was born in Logan County, KY, in 1801. Conducting dedicated Sacrament services was the central focal point of the Red River awakening and a tradition we should heed at this hour.

The views and attitudes of church leaders towards Communion in the great awakening of the mid-1700s also played a role in the ministry and church of Jonathan Edwards in 1739, but for a less positive reason. Their compromise regarding Communion and the Halfway Covenant was detrimental and is being repeated in some denominations today.

To me, the greatest awakening that ever took place in church history was on the Day of Pentecost when thousands repented of their sins and were baptized in water. Along with water baptism, Communion immediately became a foundational component for all believers and in establishing the new church.

The experiences the apostles had with Jesus over the previous three years and the Lord's institution of Communion in His last Passover were challenging. For three years, they had listened to Jesus' teachings and were now struggling to understand all he was telling them about the upcoming events regarding his death and resurrection.

I think they had difficulty comprehending the Lord's revelation of the New Covenant Communion and what it would mean for all of them. However, after His resurrection, a profound change occurred. Jesus made several appearances and showed Himself alive by many infallible proofs, being seen by them for forty days and speaking of things pertaining to the kingdom of God. (Acts 1:3)

From the resurrection and throughout those forty days, the apostles' understanding of Communion and the Lord's teachings on the Kingdom of God would surely expand exponentially. This expansion of understanding was not just for their personal growth but to prepare them for what was coming on the Day of Pentecost and for the missions ahead of them.

This sense of anticipation, of being prepared for the

tasks ahead, is one that we should all embrace in our own lives.

After spending ten days praying in one accord in the upper room, the Lord poured out the Holy Spirit. They were all filled with the Holy Spirit and began to speak in other tongues as the Spirit gave them utterance. This event's unity and shared experience must have been profound, as everyone on the streets below the upper room heard them. The Bible tells us in Acts 2 how these people responded to what they heard.

They were confused, amazed, perplexed, and some mocked them. But Peter stood and preached a message that cut so deep into their hearts that the people asked him what they needed to do. Peter told them to repent and be baptized in the name of Jesus Christ for the remission of sins. That day, about three thousand people were saved, and the church began to grow.

Communion After Pentecost

From Passover to Pentecost, the awakening had evolved to fruition, and the New Covenant Communion was introduced to all new believers with an immediate and lasting impact. It was so powerful that they received Communion daily and from house to house. The first awakening was well underway, and Holy Communion was placed as a foundational ordinance for the church and all believers.

When the fullness of time had come to establish His church, they not only had Communion, also known as the breaking of bread, but they continued having it daily and from house to house.

This is of great importance today. Too many believers think that having Communion once a week at church is enough, but I believe the Lord is calling us to engage in Communion in our personal lives throughout the week.

The early church shows us how serious they were regarding Communion, and the powerful results speak for themselves. They had a new and very complete understanding of this New Covenant Communion because the Apostles were teaching it to them.

> *And they continued steadfastly in the apostles' doctrine and fellowship, in the **breaking of bread**, and in prayers. [43] Then fear came upon every soul, and many wonders and signs were done through the apostles. - Acts 2:42-43 NKJV*

> *[46] So **continuing daily** with one accord in the temple, and **breaking bread** from house to*

house, they ate their food with gladness and simplicity of heart, [47] praising God and having favor with all the people. And the Lord added to the church daily those who were being saved. - Acts 2:46-47 NKJV

There is a pattern we should consider returning to. They were steadfast in the doctrine and in fellowship. They were steadfast in breaking bread and in prayer. Again, the results are indisputable, and many wonders and signs were done by the apostles.

Today, we are seeing a greater emphasis on prayer, and many from around the world have responded to the call. God is calling us to encounter Him individually and often in Communion. The results of answered prayer, salvations, signs, and wonders will increase dramatically, and your intimacy with the Lord will be precious.

The Scriptures reinforce that they continued daily with one accord in the temple. The Lord is calling us to drop our differences, stop debating, and gather around the body and blood of Jesus. We must acknowledge that we are one body of Christ with many members. When we stand as one in Him while holding the bread and cup in our hands, we will humbly pray to the Father, and He will be pleased.

As they continued to break bread from house to

house, praising God and receiving favor with all the people, there were daily salvations, and many were added to the church. They immediately became a part of the church, not just a list of names for follow-up. These people truly experienced repentance and the salvation of God with a heart's desire to be part of the church. There is power in Communion!

The more frequently believers partake in personal Communion, the more aware they will be of their covenant blessings, His leadings, and presence with a more intimate relationship with God, all of which leads to a more significant impact on church gatherings and services. Scripture clearly outlines this pattern, and we need to follow it.

The first great awakening in Jerusalem happened when it did because it was the time God had chosen. It was a Kairos moment. In the fullness of time, God brought forth His Son as the Lamb of God to be offered for the sins of the world.

From the Lord's Last Supper at the Passover to the Day of Pentecost, these events took place at a time selected by God Himself, and its success was found in the Lord's obedience to do the Father's will.

We have been given a specific opportunity, a moment in time. God is entrusting us with this unique moment in history to steward the challenges and the outpourings of our day. Communion Encounters Services are upon us. Let's do it right and not follow the pattern of the North Hampton, MA churches during the mid-1700s.

Communion - First Great Awakening in America (1730s – 1760s)

What historians call the First Great Awakening through the American colonies was more a revitalization of religious piety and a pivotal period in American history, with its most significant years from 1739 to 1742. It was a series of revivals that spread through the colonies, leaving an indelible mark. Key figures such as Jonathan Edwards, George Whitefield, and John and Charles Wesley played instrumental roles in this transformative period.

Unlike the Second Great Awakening, which reached the unchurched, this movement was a pronounced shift and challenge for those who were already church members.

In the 1630s, Puritans arrived in America to build a biblical society free from the Church of England and to be an example to the nations. This generation followed God closely, and Communion (Holy Sacraments) was taken seriously. Communion was a carryover from Scotland and England and was brought to the colonies.

However, as time passed, the enthusiasm waned. The once fervent faith in God, as the center of their lives, began to fade, and the Lord no longer held their hearts.

The significance of communion, once a cornerstone of their faith, diminished. The 'Age of Reason' ushered in an era of self-reliance and self-indulgence, where they believed they could manage their lives independently of God.

People had forgotten God and lost their fear of Him. Focused on prosperity, immorality, and drunkenness, they indulged in excessive sexual pleasures. Those who externally appeared to live for God had lost their hearts for Him. All these things combined were causing church roles to dry up, and ministers had to do something. Does this sound familiar?

Many North American churches and denominations today face a similar predicament. The Word of God no longer dictates their lives, and a false narrative that God accepts people as they are, allowing them to live a sinful life, has taken root. This narrative contradicts God's message of repentance and eternal life to all sinners.

This false narrative has deceived many. Church attendance has been decreasing for years, and church leaders have made numerous compromises to lure people to attend their services. For many, church growth was not about repenting of sin and having a relationship with Jesus Christ. Instead, they ignored the Word of God, lived how they wanted, and canceled those who disagreed.

Today, we see how church leaders have compromised with the Word of God to the point that sometimes, I wonder if the leaders are saved. The blind are leading the blind, and this is the same as in the First Great Awakening. The leaders took wrong and drastic action to get the world to attend their church services.

The Halfway Covenant

The Halfway Covenant was created in 1662 in the Massachusetts colony. Church attendance was very low, and people had lost interest in church and God. Therefore, the leaders created the halfway covenant that would not require a public profession of faith for salvation and, hopefully, would drive up church attendance and membership.

It was a country club mentality to come as you are, and sadly, no one would say anything or question you regarding your relationship with God. This allowed church membership without being born again!

We see this today in many denominations where

sinful, unrepenting lifestyles are acceptable in the name of attendance and money.

Halfway members soon outnumbered true believers, and they were socially acceptable since they were not religious fanatics. They were allowed to live in sin and come to church to perform their religious duty while living a lie.

When the halfway covenant began, they could not partake in Communion, but eventually, they were allowed. Over time, they ignored the Scripture about taking Communion in an unworthy manner altogether. This compromise led to a more significant compromise. They decided that the halfway covenant members could go into the ministry. They weren't saved, but it was a promising career. The lost started leading the lost! Something needed to happen as Christianity was being threatened.

Jonathan Edwards Deals With The Halfway Covenant

In 1727, Jonathan was a co-pastor with his grandfather, Solomon Stoddard. Jonathan challenged the halfway covenant members, their dead works, and their church membership. He preached a strong message of justification by faith and not of works. He clearly told them they must be born again.

A Time Of Awakening

After eight years, revival broke out at his Northampton church in 1735. The faith and prayers of godly leaders were suddenly being answered. (That's encouraging. Keep praying, our "suddenly" is coming.) The Spirit of God began to bring people out of their slumber, and many began to experience revival and awakening, with many salvations.

However, the Northampton Church continued to embrace the halfway covenant and began allowing unconverted people to partake in Holy Communion. Jonathan's Grandfather, Solomon Stoddard, believed the Lord's Supper could be a converting ordinance and encouraged the lost to partake of the Sacraments as it might bring people to Christ. He was wrong.

Jonathan believed it was for born-again Christians only. He also preached that partaking in Holy Communion in their lost state would do nothing for them other than bring them into judgment.

Over time, disagreements grew over who could or could not participate in Communion, leading to division over maintaining the halfway covenant. Jonathan worked to change this over time, but a significant dispute finally took place, and Jonathan Edwards was dismissed in 1750 after serving as the pastor for 23 years. He died in January 1758, shortly after becoming the President of Princeton.

In looking at the impact of Communion in this awakening, we can see that Jonathan took a solid stand for the Word of God. His influence on this Awakening was tremendous. There was a clear divide between darkness and light, and the compromise of God's truth was prevalent.

Unfortunately, the battle was within the organized church, much like today. We must look at the areas of compromise around Communion in our churches and make the changes. We must, once again, approach Communion as Holy and Sacred with a goal of greater intimacy with the Father, Son, and Holy Spirit like never before. Personal Communion on a very regular basis will bring us to a greater realization of His presence and Glory. It is my goal to help you get there through this book.

We are in a window of opportune times that must not be ignored. The Communion Encounter Reformation for believers and churches has been born. We must now engage it in faith that the Awakening and harvest of souls the Father desires is coming.

NOW IS THE TIME. IT IS OUR MOMENT!

Chapter 2

Communions Impact On Past Awakening

You may already know a lot about the Second Great Awakening, which started at Red River in Logan County, Kentucky, and then moved across Kentucky to Cain Ridge in Paris the following year. Over that time, there were many Sacrament Events that drew thousands of people to each one.

The Lord is using these historical events to speak to us in this moment. We must learn about the past and allow the Holy Spirit to guide us into the next awakening, with Communion at its heart. I know what the Lord has spoken to me, and I believe we can draw insights from history that will enlighten our path forward.

The Second Great Awakening occurred from 1796 to 1835 in Kentucky and is of great importance to what is happening today regarding Communion.

Second Great Awakening in America (1796 – 1835)

Throughout the 1700s, the churches placed great importance on the Holy Sacraments, which carried over into the 1800s. The Presbyterians, in particular, held annual Holy Sacrament or Holy Fair events that lasted four to nine days and were usually outdoors. Because it was an annual event, large crowds would gather.

However, circuit preachers traveling through the wilderness or those who pastored small churches emphasized regularly partaking in the Holy Sacraments, as they understood their need and the power in Communion.

Methodist circuit preachers rode thousands of miles on horseback to establish churches in remote settlements. Presbyterian, Methodist, and Baptist preachers traveled through the wilderness preaching and bringing the Sacraments wherever possible.

James McGeady made partaking in the Holy Sacraments a significant focus in his three churches, second only to prayer. It was in the local church Sacrament services that revival and awakening would begin and then explode into the Second Great Awakening in June 1800. But how did it start? What was the trigger?

Red River

In 1796, revivalist James McGready arrived in Logan County, KY, traveling by horseback as a circuit preacher. In January 1797, he began leading three small churches, the Red River, the Gasper River, and the Muddy River churches, which would later birth the Second Great Awakening. These congregations were initially small and had little religious interest.

McGready was stunned by the coldness of church people towards religion and saw they were going through the motions. There was no anointing or presence of God in the services, and many just stayed home and disengaged. Sound familiar yet?

In some ways, our world today is not only cold towards religion as it was then, but we are also seeing a greater hostility towards Christianity in general. Whole denominations have compromised the Word of God, embraced anti-biblical doctrines, and removed passages or denied their relevance in today's society or for their church.

And yet, revival fires are springing up in many places around the world and on college campuses, and water baptisms are also increasing.

After seeing the deadness of the church, McGready created a preamble that committed them to set times of prayer and fasts for one year. He also committed to having regular Holy Sacrament services at each church. One year later, the awakening was born.

Communion Encounters

As we pray for our communities and nation, we will continue to conduct Communion Encounter services in churches and communities. We have been given a window of opportunity, and it's time to advance.

I see a parallel from that time to what is happening today.

The Lord has raised up nationwide intercessory prayer groups with Holy Spirit-led coordination in every state in America. More people are also fasting, and whole churches are now engaged in regular times of corporate prayer and fasting. They are preparing the stage for a powerful awakening, leading to a tremendous harvest of souls that will impact entire communities and nations. The fires are burning, and more will be lit.

The Preamble & Covenant

In 1796, McGready presented the following preamble and covenant to the members of his congregation for their approval and signatures. People from all three churches signed and carried it out.

> *When we consider the word and promises of a compassionate God to the poor lost family of Adam, we find the strongest encouragement for Christians to pray in*

faith, to ask in the name of Jesus for the conversion of their fellow man.

None ever went to Christ when on earth, with the case of their friends, that were denied, and, although the days of his humiliation are ended, yet for the encouragement of his people, he has left it on record that where two or three agree upon earth to ask in prayer, believing, it shall be done. Again, whatsoever you shall ask the Father in my name, that will I do, that the Father may be glorified in the Son.

With these promises before us, we feel encouraged to unite our supplications to a prayer-hearing God for the outpouring of his Spirit, that his people may be quickened and comforted, and that our children, and sinners generally, may be converted.

Therefore, we bind ourselves to observe the third Saturday of each month, for one year, as a day of fasting and prayer for the conversion of sinners in Logan County and throughout the world.

We also engage to spend one-half hour every Saturday evening, beginning at the setting of the sun, and one-half hour every Sabbath morning, from the rising of the sun, pleading with God to revive his work.

Their commitment to this preamble and covenant of prayer triggered the Second Great Awakening.

Between 1796 and June 1800, McGready traveled to his three churches and continued to exhort the church to pray for the lost and backslidden. He would conduct Holy Sacrament Services regularly, and it was in one of these services at Gasper River, that God began to pour out His Spirit.

From McGready's Journal

While his journal is lengthy, I have selected a few entries that tell the story from his own words. Three things stand out in his journal. Prayer, fasting, and the Sacrament Services. It was during the Sacrament services, in particular, that the most remarkable outpourings occurred. This is especially true at the Red River Sacrament event in June 1800. The awakening was birthed in the Sacrament Meetings!

During a Sacrament meeting on a Monday in May 1797, the first signs of revival started when a young lady accepted Jesus and was born again, and many came under great conviction and awareness of their sin. Here are a few of his journal entries.

A Time Of Awakening

May 1797 (Gasper River) – "A universal deadness and stupidity prevailed in these congregations till the May following when the Lord visited the Gasper River congregation with an outpouring of his Spirit. A very considerable number, both men and women, were awakened to a deep and solemn sense of their sin and danger."

Winter 1797-1798 (Gasper River) – "During the winter, a general declension seemed to take place; coldness and deadness overspread the congregation; this struck a general alarm to all praying Christians. The people of God were painfully exercised about the perishing state of sinners and sorely distressed under the gloomy appearance of the Spirit's withdrawing and the work of God ceases. *Particular times were set apart for prayer, and the last Saturday in each month was set apart as a day of fasting and prayer to God for the church of Christ.*"

07.28.1799 (Red River) – "In this dismal state of deadness and darkness, our congregations lay until the fourth Sabbath in July 1799, when *the Sacrament of the Lord's Supper was administered at Red River.*"

09.29.1799 (Muddy River) – "On the 5th

Sabbath of September, *the Sacrament of the Supper was administered at Muddy River*. This has generally been considered the greatest, the most solemn, and powerful time of any that had been heretofore. Every day of the occasion was marked with visible tokens of God's presence. At this time, many persons were solemnly awakened, and many distressed souls were relieved by sweet, soul-satisfying views of Jesus."

"It was a time of unspeakable comfort, joy, and peace among God's people; many of them feasted on the hidden manna and felt the very dawning of Heaven in their souls; they had sweet nearness and access to God and found it easy to hold up the state of the church, the case of distressed awakened souls, and the pitiable conditions of poor, unconverted sinners, before God."

06.15.1800 (Red River) – "The *first extraordinary manifestation of divine power was at Red River, where the Sacrament of the Supper was administered on the third Sabbath of June.* This was indeed a blessed day of the Son of Man—The Lord afforded more than common light, life, and zeal to his ministers, and more than common life to the exercise of his praying people."

"Upon every day of the occasion, there were visible tokens of the love and goodness of God. Christians were filled with joy and peace in believing, and poor, distressed, condemned sinners were brought to see the glory and fullness of a crucified Jesus and to feel the power and efficacy of his merits and atonement."

McGready saw the connection between the Sacrament season and revival. He recorded in his journal in 1800 that 16 of 17 revivals occurred from Sacrament Meetings and spread throughout the frontier.

A Communion reformation and awakening is happening again now.

Three Years Later – Red River Explodes

On June 13-17, 1800, McGready held the Red River Sacrament as a traditional Presbyterian event. This became a substantial ecumenical event with Presbyterian, Methodist, and Baptist preachers working together throughout the crowds. People came from many miles in covered wagons and on horses or mules. Campsites were set up, and ministry occurred around the clock as God poured out His Spirit. This is where the term "Camp Meeting" first got its name.

Communion Encounters

Communion had turned into an ecumenical, evangelical awakening in the hearts of the believers and the lost!

This awakening then spread across multiple states and is still inspiring us today. It also significantly impacted Barton Stone, the Presbyterian pastor of the Cain Ridge Church in Paris, KY, northeast of Lexington, KY, and would set the course for the Cain Ridge Awakening in 1801.

Barton Stone wrote a letter describing his experience at Red River.

> *"There on the edge of a prairie in Logan County, Kentucky, the multitudes came together and continued a number of days and nights encamped on the ground, during which time worship was carried on in some part of the encampment. The scene was new to me and passing strange. It baffled description. Many, very many, fell down as men slain in battle and continued for hours together in an apparently breathless and motionless state, sometimes for a few moments reviving and exhibiting symptoms of life by a deep groan or piercing shriek, or by a prayer for mercy fervently uttered. After lying there for hours, they obtained deliverance. The gloom cloud that had*

covered their faces seemed gradually and visibly to disappear, and hope, in smiles, brightened into joy."

"They would rise, shouting deliverance, and then would address the surrounding multitude in language truly eloquent and impressive. With astonishment did I hear men, women, and children declaring the wonderful works of God and the glorious mysteries of the gospel. Their appeals were solemn, heart-penetrating, bold, and free. Under such circumstances, many others would fall down into the same state from which the speakers had just been delivered."

Cain Ridge - Aug 1801 Communion Event

The Red River Sacrament event was contagious. Barton Stone went to Red River and visited other Sacramental Communion events to promote the Cain Ridge event he was holding in August 1801. Many people do not know about all the Sacramental Communion Events preceding Cain Ridge, which was 14 months after Red River.

From the Red River event, awakening spread across Tennessee, North and South Carolina, and Virginia. Sacramental Communion events spread across Kentucky and were held ahead of Cain Ridge. They included Concord, with over 4,000 people; Lexington, with 6,000 people; and Indian Creek, with over 10,000. Barton Stone networked with all of them, starting at Red River to let everyone know he was having a Sacramental meeting beginning Friday, August 8, and ending on August 13, 1801.

Military personnel estimated the crowds to be between 20,000 and 30,000 for the entire event. For the serving of Communion on Sunday, over 12,000 people arrived in over 125 wagons, eight carriages, and untold numbers of horses and mules. Trees were cut down to make room for the wagons and campsites. The crowd kept building.

In a totally ecumenical setting, preachers from all the different denominations preached nonstop, day and night. People stayed through the week and did not leave until they had run out of supplies for themselves and their horses.

The eyewitness accounts are amazing. The physical manifestations of God's Spirit were remarkable. Many fell to the ground under the burden of their sin and cried for mercy. One person wrote that over 500 people gathered on a hill suddenly fell to the ground like they had been shot.

Many began to cry out for God's mercy while others lay on the ground like they were passed out. Great joy came upon people as they had received salvation. Many others lay on the ground shaking, and others were filled with the Holy Spirit and began to speak in tongues like it was the day of Pentecost. Revival is messy, unorganized, and seemingly out of control. Awesome.

Colonel Robert Patterson wrote a letter to Rev. Doctor John King on September 25, 1801. Here are some excerpts from his letter.

> *"As well as I am able, I will describe the emotion. Of all ages, from 8 years old and upwards, male and female, rich and poor, the blacks and of every denomination, those in favor of it, as well as those, at the instant in opposition to it, and railing against it, have instantaneously laid motionless on the ground. Some feel the approaching symptoms by being under deep conviction; their heart swells, their nerves relax, and in an instant, they become motionless and speechless but generally retain their senses."*

> *"Suppose so large a congregation assembled in the woods, ministers preaching day and night, the camp illuminated with candles, on trees, on wagons, and at the tents. People were falling down and carried out of the crowd by those next to them and taken to*

some convenient place where prayer was made for them. If they speak, what they say is attended to, being very solemn as many are struck under such exhortations. Now suppose twenty of these groups around, some rejoicing and great solemnity on every countenance."

Religious fervor and church membership soared. Multiple denominations started along with hundreds of churches and many Bible Colleges. The Communion birthed Awakening, which also brought black and white people together.

In the churches, the slaves and their owners were treated as equals because they were brothers and sisters in Christ. Historical Church records show all races were treated the same when it came to church membership, and this would have an impact on the Civil War and the fight to end slavery.

God is using me to share a message regarding individual and corporate Communion and the needed Communion Reformation in the body of Christ.

Our services have already impacted pastors, churches, and individuals, helping them understand a much greater depth of Holy Communion and approach it with honor as a Holy and Sacred ordinance rather than just a quick routine in church.

A Time Of Awakening

We have witnessed miracles, healings, and lives simply transformed.

In one Communion Encounter service, a woman holding the bread and the cup in her hands came to the altar to speak with me and asked me to pray for her. She told me she had been raised in church and had taken Communion many times before, but during my message and invitation, she realized she was lost and had never been born again.

She said the teaching on Communion had opened her eyes to this reality, and she had accepted Jesus as her Lord and Savior while sitting in her seat. That's the power of Communion. The hearts are revealed, and it's becoming more personal and intimate with Jesus.

We cannot ignore the voice of God calling us into this Communion Reformation and Awakening. Our calling is clear, and I am sounding the alarm as our time has come. Let us gather around the Holy Sacrament of Communion and let the Lord's will be done so we may host His presence and be His habitation.

Communion Encounters

Chapter 3

The Cups Of Communion

There are four cups in *The Passover*. When Jesus had His last Passover with the disciples, there would have been all four cups. Two of them are mentioned in Luke 22 and are of great significance. However, in I Corinthians 11, Paul tells us that Jesus gave him a revelation of Communion, but it only included one particular cup, which is the most important cup of all.

There is minimal teaching on Communion in churches today. Most churches observe it monthly, and others have it weekly. In many church services, Communion is nothing more than a box to check in the service outline.

For most churches, Communion rarely lasts more than 10 minutes and is so somber and limiting to the believer's interaction with Jesus that they walk away feeling something is still missing. Their experience was hollow and only focused on Jesus's death and suffering.

The Lord wants us to experience the fullness of Life in Communion and, once again, see it for what it is: Holy and Sacred. We must once again approach it with that in our hearts.

In Luke 22, Jesus presented two cups, the first in verse 17 and the second in verse 20. In I Corinthians 11:25, Paul shares about one cup. Matthew and Mark also mention only one cup.

Jesus Institutes the Lord's Supper – With Two Cups

> *[14] When the hour had come, He sat down, and the twelve apostles with Him. [15] Then He said to them, "With fervent desire, I have desired to eat this Passover with you before I suffer; [16] for I say to you, I will no longer eat of it until it is fulfilled in the kingdom of God."*
>
> *[17] **Then He took the cup**, gave thanks, and said, "Take this and divide it among yourselves; [18] for I say to you, I will not drink of the fruit of the vine until the kingdom of God comes." [19] And He took bread, gave thanks and broke it, and gave it to them, saying, "This is My body which is given for you; do this in remembrance of Me."*
>
> *[20] Likewise, **He also took the cup after supper**, saying, "This cup is the new covenant in My blood, which is shed for you.* Luke 22:14-20 NKJV

A Time Of Awakening

The Four Cups of Passover

Jesus was having Passover, and it included four cups. The two cups Jesus presented in Luke 22 are the second cup, which is the cup of deliverance, and the third cup, which is the cup of redemption. Each had a particular meaning and is now combined in the single cup we drink in Communion today. When Jesus picked up the second cup, He made a profound declaration. He said, *"This cup is the new covenant in My blood."*

He announced the fulfillment of the old covenant and the law and clearly stated that a new covenant was in the Cup of His blood. We will dig deeper into this in later chapters, but for now, let's make one crucial point: The four cups of Passover are now combined into one cup: the Cup of the New Covenant in the blood of Jesus, which we drink.

To better understand the four cups, look at Exodus 6:6-8 for the answers and learn how this applies to us in Communion.

> *6 Therefore, say to the children of Israel: 'I am the LORD; I will bring you out from under the burdens of the Egyptians, I will rescue you from their bondage, and I will redeem you with an outstretched arm and with great judgments. 7 I will take you as My*

> *people, and I will be your God. Then you*
> *shall know that I am the LORD your God who*
> *brings you out from under the burdens of the*
> *Egyptians. [8] And I will bring you into the land*
> *which I swore to give to Abraham, Isaac, and*
> *Jacob; and I will give it to you as a heritage:*
> *I am the LORD.'"* - Exodus 6:6-8 NKJV

First Cup: The Cup of Sanctification. *I will bring you out from under your burdens.* (Verse 6)

After 430 years, the Lord is bringing them out of their bondage and the burden of slavery, which, for mankind, is related to the bondage to sin and its heavy burden.

However, we have Jesus as our Passover, and by his blood, we are cleansed from sin and sanctified. We are delivered, redeemed, and adopted as children of Almighty God, who is now our heavenly Father.

The language "bring you out" and the definition of sanctification are significant. They were brought out and set apart into the promised land.

In Greek, the word *hagiazo* is translated as sanctification. It means to make holy, purify, and sanctify, to be separate from profane things and dedicated and consecrated to God. It is to be free from the guilt of sin and to be pure internally. This can only be accomplished through the shed blood of Jesus applied to our lives.

To increase your intimacy with Jesus in Communion and release and appropriate the Covenant Blessings, I will share throughout this book various definitions and decrees that you can make during your time of Communion. Consider each verse and then incorporate the decree as you drink the Cup.

> *By that will we have been sanctified through the offering of the body of Jesus Christ once for all. [14]For by one offering He has perfected forever those who are being sanctified. -* Hebrews 10:10, 14 NKJV

When we prepare to partake of the cup in Communion, we can use this and the other Scriptures to make powerful declarations. You can say something like this.

> *"Father, I proclaim that I have been sanctified through the body and blood of Jesus as your Passover Lamb, and He has perfected me forever by His blood, and I continue to receive the ongoing sanctification of my life in spirit, soul, and body for your glory."*

Here is another verse on sanctification.

And such were some of you. But you were washed, but you were sanctified, but you were justified in the name of the Lord Jesus and by the Spirit of our God. - I Corinthians 6:11 NKJV

We are washed, cleansed, and sanctified by Jesus's blood! You can use this verse to decree something like the following.

I have been washed and cleansed of my sins. I am free! I have been sanctified and justified in the name of the Lord Jesus and by the Spirit of my God and Heavenly Father.

Consider another very powerful Scripture in II Corinthians 6 and its decree.

And what agreement has the temple of God with idols? For you are the temple of the living God. As God has said, "I will dwell in them and walk among them. I will be their God, and they shall be My people." [17] Therefore, "<u>Come out from among them and be separate</u>, says the Lord. Do not touch what is unclean, and I will receive you. [18] I will be a Father to you, and you shall be My sons and daughters, says the Lord Almighty." - II Cor 6:16-18 NKJV

A Time Of Awakening

Now, we can use these verses and make another powerful decree as we drink the cup of the new covenant in His blood. Declare it to Him and acknowledge Him as you make your decree.

> *I am the temple of the living God, my heavenly Father. The Father, Son, and Holy Spirit dwell in me and walk with me at all times. Therefore, I separate myself from the things of this world that could lead me into sin, and I draw near to my Heavenly Father. He receives me and fellowships with me. My heart is full of assurance that God is my Father, and I am His child by the blood of Jesus. Thank you, Jesus!*

Second Cup: The Cup of Deliverance – *I will rescue you from your burdens* (verse 6)

We can only imagine the agony the children of Israel carried for 430 years. Multiple generations were born and died in misery. They were treated with cruelty and cried out to God for their deliverance. In Exodus 3:7, God told Moses he had seen the oppression of His people in Egypt and had heard their cries because of the sorrows their taskmasters brought on them. He told Moses He was ready to deliver them with a mighty outstretched arm and bring them into the promised land flowing with milk and honey.

What He spoke to Moses was from the Covenant He made with Abram in Genesis.

> *13 Then He said to Abram: "Know certain that your descendants will be strangers in a land that is not theirs, and will serve them, and they will afflict them four hundred years. 14 And also the nation whom they serve I will judge; afterward, they shall come out with great possessions.* – Genesis 15:13-14 NKJV

Israel's deliverance is celebrated in Passover in the Cup of Deliverance. Our deliverance should and can be celebrated and remembered in the Cup of the New Covenant in the Blood of Jesus every time we drink it.

As we look at the following Scriptures, we will renew our minds in God's truth and again appropriate and decree the power of deliverance in His blood. I also want to encourage you to make these decrees when you are having Communion.

While it would be a remarkable transformation in the church services to make decrees during Communion, I highly encourage you to do this in your personal Communion and prayer times. You will experience the intimacy and presence of the Lord in more excellent dimensions as you do. Take your time.

A Time Of Awakening

Meditate on the Scripture, take sips of the cup, and appropriate the blessings in the blood of Christ as you do.

Consider these Scriptures.

> *Grace to you and peace from God the Father and our Lord Jesus Christ, [4] who gave Himself for our sins that He might deliver us from this present evil age, according to the will of our God and Father, [5] to whom be glory forever and ever. Amen.* - Galatians1:3-5 NKJV

> *He has delivered us from the power of darkness and conveyed us into the kingdom of the Son of His love, [14] in whom we have redemption through His blood, the forgiveness of sins.* - Colossians 1:13-14 NKJV

Let's combine these into one decisive decree and appropriation of the blood of Jesus.

> *I receive and acknowledge the grace, the undeserved kindness, and total well-being in the peace of my Heavenly Father and my Lord Jesus Christ, who gave Himself for my sins and who has delivered me from the present evil and worldly age according to the*

will of my God and Heavenly Father.

The blood of Jesus has completely delivered me from the rule, influence, and powers of darkness at all levels and conveyed me into the Kingdom of the Son of the Father's love. In Him, I now have redemption through His blood and the forgiveness of sins. Thank you, Father, for this beautiful covenant blessing in my life.

Third Cup: The Cup of Redemption - *I will redeem you; I will bless you.* (verse 6)

The power in this cup excites me the most. I am redeemed! In Exodus 12, the Lord explained the Passover and precisely what He would do to deliver Israel from Egypt. This chapter is full of revelation, but let's focus on one verse related to the third cup and our redemption through the blood of Jesus.

> *Now, the blood shall be a sign for you on the houses where you are. And <u>when I see the blood</u>, I will pass over you; and the plague shall not be on you to destroy you when I strike the land of Egypt.* - Exodus 12:13 NKJV

The Lord said the blood would be a sign, and when He would see the blood applied to the doorpost and the lintel, He would PASS OVER them, and the plague would not destroy them even though it was all around them! When the blood is applied to our lives under the new covenant, we are cleansed, made whole, and protected. That is the power of appropriation in faith and authority.

This gives us a greater understanding of blood sacrifices and the blood covenant. Sacrifice was a means of deliverance and protection for the individual, the family, and the whole nation, but only when the blood was applied.

The blood of sacrificial animals was used as an offering for sins and consecration. This was first called the blood of the covenant in Exodus 24:4-8. (*In a later chapter, we will look more deeply at the Blood Covenant and the significance of what Jesus said concerning the "Cup of the new COVENANT in His blood.)*

We see more details about blood sacrifices in the Mosaic covenant and the Levitical priesthood. In these blood sacrifices, the life of the animal was sacrificed for another life. It was a life for a life, but its blood only covered sin and never cleansed people of sin, which we now have because of Jesus as the Lamb of God and His sacrifice. The power of Jesus's blood has redeemed us. Jesus purchased our lives. He gave us His life so we could have His eternal life.

Communion Encounters

During Holy Communion, and the drinking of the Cup of the New Covenant in His blood, knowing and acknowledging that we are redeemed should humble us, fill our hearts with gratitude and joy, and fill our mouths with thanksgiving and rejoicing.

Let's look at some powerful Scriptures that can be used to release the power of the Cup of the New Covenant in His blood.

> *Christ has redeemed us from the curse of the law, having become a curse for us (for it is written, "Cursed is everyone who hangs on a tree"), [14] that the blessing of Abraham might come upon the Gentiles in Christ Jesus, that we might receive the promise of the Spirit through faith.* - Galatians 3:13-14 NKJV

> *Knowing that you were not redeemed with corruptible things, like silver or gold, from your aimless conduct received by tradition from your fathers, [19] but with the precious blood of Christ, as of a lamb without blemish and without spot.* - I Peter 1:18-19 NKJV

> *Who gave Himself for us, that He might redeem us from every lawless deed and purify for Himself His own special people, zealous for good works.* - Titus 2:14 NKJV

For it pleased the Father that in Him all the fullness should dwell, [20] and by Him to reconcile all things to Himself, by Him, whether things on earth or things in heaven, having made peace through the blood of His cross. - Colossians 1:19-20 NKJV

Let the redeemed of the LORD say so, whom He has redeemed from the hand of the enemy. - Psalm 107:2 NKJV

Once again, let's combine these into one decisive decree and appropriation of the blood of Jesus while drinking the cup of Communion. Acknowledge the Lord's presence as you do this.

Because Jesus Christ has redeemed me from the curse of the law, the blessing of Abraham is continually coming upon me as I am in Christ Jesus, and I have the promise of the Spirit in and upon me now.

I acknowledge that I was not redeemed by the corruptible things of this world, but I have been redeemed by the precious blood of Christ, who was God's Lamb, without blemish or spot.

Jesus gave Himself for me so that He could redeem me and purify me for Himself as a special person who

is zealous for good works that will glorify Him.

All the fullness of God dwells in Jesus, and He has reconciled me to Himself, and I now have peace through the blood of His cross.

I am the redeemed of the Lord who has redeemed me from the hand of the enemy!

More About The Third Cup

The Cup of Redemption is also called the Cup of Blessing. Only one verse in the Bible refers to the third cup as the cup of blessing. Remember, this is the second cup Jesus presented in Luke 22 and the only one in I Corinthians 11.

> *The cup of blessing which we bless, is it not the Communion of the blood of Christ? The bread which we break, is it not the Communion of the body of Christ?* - I Corinthians 10:16 NKJV

The key word is Communion, and the Greek word is Koinonia, commonly translated as fellowship. However, Koinonia has a much deeper meaning and is very revealing in this verse. It also means partnership, participation, and intimacy.

By using this word, Paul makes it clear that "Communion" has a profound meaning. When the

Lord led me to this, and after I had researched the word more deeply, He spoke the following to me. It is very revealing as to what we should experience with Him in Communion.

> *"The cup of blessing which we bless, is it not an intimate participation in partnership with the blood of Jesus? The bread which we break, is it not an intimate participation in partnership with the body of Christ?"* - I Corinthians 10:16 NKJV.

Yes, it is! Meditate on those words as you eat the bread and drink from the cup.

It is a time of intimacy and participation with Jesus in total partnership. We are one with Him. Enjoy your time with Him.

Fourth Cup: The Cup of Praise – *I will take you as My People and be your God*. (verse 6)

Traditional Passovers end with the reading or singing of Psalms 113 through Psalm 118. They would sing hymns, as recorded in Mark 14:26. After the Passover, they sang a hymn and went to the Mount of Olives, where Jesus was about to be arrested. Jesus was under a very heavy burden, and there is no record that they drank the fourth cup of praise.

Communion Encounters

Most of the time, when we have Communion privately or at church, it is very serious and solemn as people focus on the Lord's sufferings and death. It's hard to have a time of praise, joy, and celebration in that atmosphere. But we must remember the whole story. He was raised from the dead, showed Himself alive by many infallible proofs, ascended to heaven, is coming again one day, and we will eventually be with Him in His glory for all eternity.

When we have Communion and remember the whole story, we will move into a time of praise, rejoicing, and celebration. We know how this ends!

So, let's establish our declaration of praise with these Scriptures. I encourage you to say them out loud when you partake of both the bread and the cup in Communion. Celebrate the whole story.

Therefore, by Him, let us continually offer the sacrifice of praise to God, that is, the fruit of our lips, giving thanks to His name. - Hebrews 13:15 NKJV

But you are a chosen generation, a royal priesthood, a holy nation, His own special people, that you may proclaim the praises of Him who called you out of darkness into His marvelous light. - I Peter 2:9 NKJV

A Time Of Awakening

I will bless the Lord at all times; His praise shall continually be in my mouth. - Psalm 34:1 NKJV

I will give You thanks in the great assembly; I will praise You among many people. - Psalm 35:18 NKJV

Great is the Lord, and greatly to be praised in the city of our God in His holy Mountain. - Psalm 48:1 NKJV

By now, I hope you see that the four cups of Passover are combined into the one Cup of the New Covenant in His Blood that Jesus presented at His last Passover. The next time you have Communion, rejoice, and celebrate Jesus. Put on a joyful, upbeat song and praise Him with a big smile on your face. You are redeemed! Act like it!!

Communion Encounters

Chapter 4

The Bread That Feeds Life

Taking Communion is the appropriation of God's life in us. That is a powerful statement, and the Holy Spirit spoke it to my heart one morning when I was having Communion. It resonated in my spirit as a powerful revelation we must embrace to gain greater intimacy with Jesus in Communion and partake of all He has given us as a result.

As we look into John 6, we see the words eternal life, live, and living several times. However, two different Greek words are translated as life, live, and living, and while uniquely connected, they bring a richer and fuller meaning to the Lord's teaching, their relationship to Communion, and their impact on our personal experience in Communion.

Two Words Defined

The first Greek word is ZOE, which you may be familiar with. It is translated as "life" and used by itself or in conjunction with "eternal life" many times.

W.E. Vine Dictionary of New Testament Words defines ZOE like this. "To have life as a principle, life in the absolute sense, life as God has it, that which the Father has in Himself and which He gave to the Incarnate Son to have in Himself.

Communion Encounters

We see this in John 5:26, *"For as the Father has (ZOE) life in Himself, so He has granted the Son to have (ZOE) life in Himself."*

The word ZOE is also used in I John 5: 12, which says, *"He who has the Son has (ZOE) life,"* which agrees with John 5:26. Jesus has the Life of God in Himself, and when we are born again, and receive the gift of eternal life, we too, have the life of God in us.

It is a powerful revelation to think we have "life as God has it" in us! That's a great life!

However, Thayer's definition is more definitive and helps us gain a deeper understanding.

Thayer describes ZOE as the state of one who has vitality, absolute fullness of life that belongs to God, a genuine active and vigorous life, is devoted to God, is blessed, and is everlasting.

The second Greek word, translated as life or living, is ZAO. This is Thayer's definition. It means to live, enjoy real life, have true life, be active, blessed, and endless in the kingdom of God, have vital power in itself and exert the same upon the soul, and be full of vigor.

These definitions are remarkable, especially when we realize how Communion releases these attributes in our lives. Let's learn how to apply this in Communion.

As we look at John 6, I have added either ZOE or ZAO in each verse as it applies. This will help you see His transition and gain a deeper understanding of what He was teaching and the depth and understanding so you can apply this to your personal Communion time.

These definitions can become your prayer and declarations as you have Communion.

Jesus' teachings concerning His body and blood were very hard to understand for them. While many of His disciples went back and walked with Him no more, the twelve stayed with Him. His teachings from that day would be more deeply revealed to the twelve during His last Passover when He presented the bread and cups of Passover and the declarations, He made concerning His flesh and His blood.

One day, many people gathered with Him and asked for a sign so they could believe in Him, saying that God had given them bread from heaven to eat. Jesus corrected them and told them that Moses did not give them bread from Heaven, *"but My Father gives you the true bread from heaven. For the bread of God is He who comes down from heaven and gives (ZOE) life to the world."* (John 6:32-33) But He did not stop there and declared in verse 35, *"I am the bread of (ZOE) life."* He is establishing a powerful truth for them.

But they still didn't understand and asked Him to always give them this bread, which Jesus answered with more revelation. *"I am the bread of (ZOE) life. He who comes to me shall never hunger, and he who believes in Me shall never thirst."* (John 6:35)

Communion Encounters

Again, He repeats the emphasis of His message in John 6:48, saying, *"I am the bread of (ZOE) life,"* and tells them when a person eats this bread, they will not die. But He put even more emphasis on His message.

Now, let's amplify the ZAO from the Thayer definition for ZAO in verse 51 to see the full impact of what Jesus said.

> *I am the (ZAO) living* (giving you a life to live, allowing you to enjoy real life, to have true life, to be active, blessed, and endless in the kingdom of God, having vital power in yourself and exerting the same upon your soul and to be full of vigor) *bread which came down from heaven. If anyone eats this bread, he will (ZAO) live forever, and the bread that I shall give is My flesh, which I shall give for the (ZOE) life of the world."* - John 6:51 NKJV

With this statement, He connected this teaching to the Holy Communion, which He would soon introduce to the apostles at His last Passover. He announced that He would give His flesh, His life, for the life of the world. Giving a life for a life is a blood covenant requirement. He introduced the New Covenant, but they did not understand it. He was the Lamb of God who would be crucified so we could have life and not die in our sins. He said whoever eats His flesh has life.

Look at how Jesus ties His flesh and His blood together and what we have as a result.

A Time Of Awakening

The following verses are precisely what we have when we partake of the Holy Sacraments in Communion.

> *Then Jesus said to them, "Most assuredly, I say to you, unless you eat the flesh of the Son of Man and drink His blood, you have no (ZOE) life in you. [54]Whoever eats My flesh and drinks My blood has eternal life, and I will raise him up at the last day.* - John 6:53-54 NKJV

This was a clear introduction to Communion and a direct correlation to His last Passover when He told them that the bread was His body, and the cup was His blood. He told them to eat the bread and drink the cup. Here, He says if a person does not do this, they have no eternal life (ZOE) in them. Those that do, have eternal life.

> [54] *Eternal life comes to the one who eats my body and drinks my blood and I will raise him up in the last day.* - John 6:54 TPT

Here is a footnote from The Passion Translation (TPT) regarding verse 54.

> To eat His flesh is to take into our life by faith all that Jesus did for us by giving His body for us. To drink His blood is to take all that the blood of Jesus has purchased for us by faith. This *eating and drinking* is receiving the life, power, and virtue of all that Jesus is to replace all that we were in Adam. Jesus' blood and body is the Tree of Life offered to everyone who follows Him.

Communion Encounters

Every time we eat the bread and drink from the cup, by faith, we feed on God's very eternal life. Our hearts are rejuvenated, uplifted, blessed, and encouraged. Sin is cleansed, bodies are healed, mental anguish is removed, and people are set free from bondages and addictions. There is power in the blood! Yes, there is still wonder-working power in the blood!

When we eat the bread and drink the cup of Communion, it is an act of faith in the natural that has Spiritual ramifications, and the Holy Spirit immediately reciprocates back to our spirit, soul, and body all that is in the Blood Covenant.

We are more aware of His presence, and there is joy, peace, and intimacy with the Lord. This is why I urge all Christians to have Communion throughout the week. Don't just do this at church on Sunday. Include Communion in your daily devotions and gain the fullness of the life He has given you, both the ZOE and ZAO life!

As you receive personal Communion more regularly, your prayer life will improve. You will begin to desire Communion and find yourself in your prayer closet more often and for extended periods of time and I know this by experience.

Partaking in the Covenant bread and blood of Jesus is the means of being joined to God and receiving the benefits of His life and the eternal life we possess through the New Birth. Jesus is the covenant sacrifice and is God's provision for our sustenance of eternal life. When we feed on the Sacraments of Communion in faith, we are feeding and partaking of God's divine nature, which is eternal life. (See II Peter 1:4)

Jesus expanded His teaching in verses 55 and 57 with two powerful truths we must know and act upon due to their importance and ongoing impact on our lives in Communion. Those two words are food and feed.

> [55] *For My flesh is **food** indeed, and My blood is **drink** indeed.* [57] *As the living Father sent Me, and I live because of the Father, so he who **feeds** on Me will live because of Me.* - John 6:55, 57 NKJV

The Passion Translation amplifies the truth that His body is food and blood is drink, by calling it REAL food and REAL drink.

> [55] *For my body is real food for your spirit, and my blood is real drink.* [56] *The one who eats my body and drinks my blood lives in me, and I live in him.* [57] *The Father of life sent me, and He is my life. In the same way, the one who feeds upon me, I will become His life.* - John 6:55-57 TPT

Jesus declares His flesh, and His blood is food. What do we do with food? We eat it and drink it, which He said in all the previous verses and His instructions at His Last Passover.

What will or should you do if you have free access to food? We FEED ON it. Where do we feed on the food and drink He has provided us? Only in the Holy Sacraments of Communion.

What is in our natural food? Vitamins, minerals, and nutrients? What is in this spiritual food of His flesh and blood? Eternal life and more life!

We had horses for many years and fed them every morning and again in the evening. We would give them grain and hay, and then they would FEED on the FOOD we gave them. It took them a while to eat everything as there was a lot to eat. Sometimes, we put them in a pasture and let them graze in the fresh green grass.

God has given us a lot of food to feed on, and we need to learn how to graze and not be in a hurry when we have Communion. Remember, you are eating and drinking eternal life and all that God has placed into it when you have Communion. Take your time when you have Communion so you can appropriate all of the God kind of life in you and enjoy His presence.

Abiding In Jesus

Jesus gave another mighty blast of revelation when He used the word abide. It is a powerful word that shows us how to remain in His presence and Communion's role. He said when we have Communion by eating the bread (His flesh) and drinking the cup (His blood), we would abide in Him, and He would abide in us.

The word abide means to dwell, remain, or remain in a given place or state of being or to continue to be present.

A Time Of Awakening

Communion is how we can continue to stay, dwell, and abide in His presence and why we must have Communion more often. It is now becoming a necessity.

> *He who eats My flesh and drinks My blood **abides** in Me, and I in him.* - John 6:56 KNJV

> *The one who eats My body and drinks My blood **lives** in Me, and I live in him.* - John 6:56 TPT

> *He that eateth My flesh, and drinketh My blood, **dwelleth** in Me and I in him.* - John 6:56 KJV

> *Anyone who eats My flesh and drinks My blood **remains** in Me, and I in him.* - John 6:56 NLT

Three Attributes of Abiding Through Communion

While there are many verses about abiding, we will stay on topic with how Communion keeps us in His abiding presence and look at what abiding through Communion can produce in our lives.

Abiding Produces Fruit

> *Abide in Me, and I in you. As the branch cannot bear fruit of itself unless it abides in the vine, neither can you unless you abide in Me. I am the vine, and you are the branches. He who abides in Me, and I in him, bears much fruit; for without Me, you can do nothing.* - John 15:4-5 KNJV

What would happen if Christians began having

Communion during their daily devotions? What would happen if more Christians took the time to have daily devotions and pray? What would happen? We would bear much fruit and glorify the Father as true disciples. (John 15: 8)

Abiding Produces Effective Prayers

> *If you abide in Me, and My words abide in you, you will ask what you desire, and it shall be done for you.* - John 15:7 NKJV

Jesus said, "if" we abide in Him. He also said if we eat His flesh and drink His blood, we will abide in Him. While we are positioned in Him through the new birth, we cannot ignore how this applies to Communion, as we have already established. Communion puts us in a place of abiding in Him, and from that place, we will pray effectively, and our prayers will be answered.

Abiding Strength To Not Sin

This next verse is a short, direct declaration about the power of abiding and victory over sin. God says we are to be Holy as He is Holy, and Communion is a significant part of this equation. The blood cleanses us, claims us, and keeps us!

> *Whoever abides in Him does not sin.* - I John 3:6 NKJV

What a powerful verse! The more I have Communion, the more I abide in Him and experience all the benefits of living in His presence. We are strengthened in the spirit and empowered to walk away from sinful temptations through Communion and His abiding presence. Through Communion, we will walk in the Spirit and not fulfill the lust of the flesh. Glory to God!

Communion Encounters

Chapter 5

This Is My Body

I grew up in a Christian home, and our family attended the First Baptist Church, which was part of the American Baptist Association. I later became very involved as a pastor in the Charismatic Full Gospel movement and a Pentecostal Denomination. I have visited many churches over the years, which has given me a wide range of observations on various topics.

One of my observations is how we do Communion in our church services, and there is very little difference. While they approach it with respect and solemnity, it has always been a small part of the service, taking less than 10 minutes from beginning to end.

As a pastor, I did the same thing. We have all followed the traditions we observed.

Whenever Communion is taken in a church service or even a home gathering, we usually read from I Corinthians 11. For the most part, churches follow the same process. We distribute the Sacraments to those who want to partake. Then, the pastor or another church leader will read from these verses, pray with thanksgiving over the bread, and then people will eat the bread. The process is then repeated for the Cup.

Depending upon where Communion is during the service, many different things happen. There is no right or wrong way or specific instruction in Scripture for how often or when we should have Communion. Jesus was clear when He said, *"As often as you do this,"* and that is our guide. Most churches then sing a song, while others move on to the rest of the service. The service may end with Communion and a closing prayer.

He Took Bread

Where did Jesus take the Bread from, and why does it matter? Why did Jesus break the bread? What did He mean when he said EAT the bread? These questions are not just rhetorical, but they are keys to unlocking a deeper understanding of Communion and its impact on our lives. Let's embark on this enlightening journey.

> *[19] And **He took bread**, gave thanks, and **broke it**, and gave it to them, saying, "**This is My body** which is given for you; do this in remembrance of Me." - Luke 22:19 NKJV*

> *For I received from the Lord that which I also delivered to you: that the Lord Jesus on*

> *the same night in which He was betrayed* **took bread***; [24] and when He had given thanks, He* **broke it** *and said,* **"Take, eat;** *this is My body which is* **broken for you;** *do this in remembrance of Me."* - I Corinthians 11:23-24 NKJV

According to many Jewish scholars and Rabbis, certain traditions regarding the Passover seder existed well before Jesus' last Passover with the Apostles. These traditions are in addition to the instructions found in Exodus 12.

Part of the Passover seder is the matzoh or unleavened bread. Three pieces of matzoh were placed inside a bag called the matzoh tosh, which had a compartment for each piece, and it was presented in a precise way during the seder. The three pieces in one bag represented unity, and there have been three views on what unity referred to.

Some Rabbis believed unity represented the unity of worship built around the High Priests, the Levites, and the people of Israel. Others say it was the unity of the Patriarchs, Abraham, Isaac, and Jacob. However, many believe, and I agree, that the three pieces represent the Trinity of the Father, the Son, and the Holy Spirit, and I believe Scripture confirms this.

The matzoh tosh is opened during the Passover seder, and the middle piece is removed and broken in half. Many Rabbis are unsure why the middle piece is broken, but the Messianic Jewish Rabbis understand it perfectly!

The broken piece is then wrapped in linen, or a linen bag called an afikomen, which means "it comes later." The afikomen is taken out of the room and hidden, symbolizing it is being buried in the house. Later, after the meal, the participants will search for the afikomen and return it to the table after it is found, with great excitement and celebration. The leader of the Passover then takes the bread, breaks it, and gives it to everyone at the table, which is what Jesus did at the Last Supper.

Let's compare the symbolism of breaking the middle piece, wrapping it in linen, hiding it, and celebrating after it is found.

The middle piece represents Jesus. When it is broken, it symbolizes Jesus being broken for us. The broken piece of matza is wrapped in linen, and Jesus was wrapped in linen. The matza was hidden, and Jesus was hidden in the tomb after His death. The afikomen, with the piece of bread, is then found and celebrated with rejoicing. Jesus was hidden from the world for three days and then celebrated with great rejoicing after His resurrection.

A Time Of Awakening

Connecting Jesus and Isaac

Jesus didn't just take any piece of the matzoh tosh; He took the middle piece and then claimed it was His body. Jesus made an amazing statement to the apostles. They knew the middle piece represented Isaac, and His proclamation would have gotten their attention. But why is this significant? The answers start in Genesis.

In Genesis 15:4, God made a covenant with Abram and promised to give him an heir from his own body. Then, in Genesis 17, God confirmed and further expanded the covenant with Abram, saying He would make Abram the father of many nations, and changed his name to Abraham. As promised, Sarah conceives, and Isaac, the promised seed of Abraham, is born.

God then makes a request of His blood covenant partner, and it will be a significant test with eternal ramifications. In blood covenant relationships, all that each partner has is available to the other party. Nothing can be withheld when the request is made, or they would be breaking the covenant.

God asked Abraham to offer up his son as a burnt offering. The stage is set. God's request was the supreme test that would demonstrate Abraham's reverence for God and his confidence that God would keep His covenant promise concerning his seed, Isaac. Abraham prepared to offer up his son with the assurance God would raise him from death. (Heb 11:19)

As Abraham and Isaac ascend the mountaintop, Isaac asks where the lamb is for the sacrifice, and Abraham tells him that God will provide Himself with the lamb for the burnt offering. After building and preparing the altar with his son as the sacrifice, God stops him with these words.

> *And He said, "Do not lay your hand on the lad, or do anything to him; for now I know that you fear God since you have not withheld your son, your only son, from Me."* - Genesis 22: 12 KNJV

This is a foreshadowing of God's offering His only Son to die in our place. Because Abraham did not withhold his son from God, God would provide His own Son as a sacrifice for the sins of the world. Jesus, the Son of God, was the Lamb of God who was slain before the foundation of the world. Abraham had exhibited his love for God, and God would show His love centuries later.

> *[13] Then Abraham lifted his eyes and looked, and there behind him was a ram caught in a thicket by its horns. So, Abraham went and*

took the ram and offered it up for a burnt offering instead of his son. [14] And Abraham called the name of the place, The-LORD-Will-Provide; as it is said to this day, "In the Mount of the LORD it shall be provided." - Genesis 22: 12-14 NKJV

[15] Then the Angel of the LORD called to Abraham a second time out of heaven, [16] and said, "By Myself, I have sworn," says the LORD, "because you have done this thing, and have not withheld your son, your only son [17] blessing I will bless you, and multiplying I will multiply your descendants as the stars of the heaven and as the sand which is on the seashore, and your descendants shall possess the gate of their enemies. [18] In your seed, all the nations of the earth shall be blessed because you have obeyed My voice." - Genesis 22:15-18 NKJV

He Broke The Bread

There are some essential things to know about unleavened bread used in the Passover. Unleavened bread is called matzah or matzo bread, and the matzo bread I use personally and in our services is also Kosher for Passover.

Scripture tells us the Israeli people left Egypt in haste

and did not have time to add the yeast and allow the bread to rise before it was baked. Because they left in haste, the bread was made only from flour and water without yeast, making the Matzah unleavened flatbread when baked.

> *33 And the Egyptians urged the people, that they might send them out of the land in haste. For they said, "We shall all be dead." 34 So the people took their dough before it was leavened, having their kneading bowls bound up in their clothes on their shoulders.* - Exodus 12:33-34 NKJV

The matzo bread has three very distinct characteristics. It has holes pierced in it as part of the baking process. It has burnt marks on it. Finally, the four edges are all burnt. The prophet Isaiah wrote about this in Isaiah 53 when writing about the Lamb of God, the Messiah.

> *Surely, he has born our griefs (sickness) and carried our sorrows (pain), yet we did esteem him stricken, smitten (struck down) of God and afflicted. (5) But he was wounded* **(pierced)** *for our transgressions (rebellion/sin), he was* **bruised** *(crushed) for our iniquities; the chastisement (discipline) of our peace was upon him; and with his* **stripes,** *we are healed.* - Isaiah 53:4-5 NKJV

A Time Of Awakening

Whenever I hold a piece of matzo bread in my hand, I look at it and meditate on its meaning. Jesus is the Lamb of God who gave His life for me. He is the Bread of Life. Holding it, I remember all He did for me because He loves me. As I eat it, I know I am eating life, not death!

First, the holes in the matzo directly refer to Jesus being wounded and pierced for our sins. Most of the time, we only think of Jesus being pierced on the cross after His death. We may also think about the nails through His hands and feet.

There was also the crown of thorns placed on His head, which would have made many painful and deep piercings into His skull, and they took a rod and beat the thorns into His head. Every time He was beaten, especially when they scourged His body with many stripes, there would be many piercings of His body as the sharp metal and bone would have done severe damage.

Second, the burnt marks on the matzo bread reflect the bruises on His body for our transgressions, which means our rebellions. The word bruised means to crush to the point of destruction. His bruises started in the garden when He was arrested and hit the first time. The beatings continued until they crucified Him.

Third, the burnt edges look like burnt stripes and represent the strips He took in the scourging for our healing. Isaiah saw this as a future event concerning the Messiah. Peter wrote about it and brought it into a past tense meaning in I Peter 2:24 when he wrote, *"By whose stripes you **were** healed."*

Eat The Bread

After Jesus took the bread, gave thanks, and broke it, He gave it to the apostles and told them to eat it. The critical focus word is now – EAT.

> *"and when He had given thanks, He **broke it** and said, "**Take, eat**; this is My body which is **broken for you**; do this in remembrance of Me."* - I Corinthians 11:23-24 NKJV

The Lord taught me how to eat the bread and drink the cup to experience Him more fully. It was life-changing and altered how I take Communion.

It started at 4:30 a.m. in prayer while having Communion. Like many people, I had been using the prepackaged communion and bread cups, but I had begun using Matzo bread and a larger glass that would have more juice than the little, hard-to-open prepackaged cups that are so popular now.

A Time Of Awakening

I was holding a small piece of the Matzo bread when the Lord prompted me to get a large piece, and then He told me to eat it. It was much too large just to put in my mouth and chew. Revelation began to flood me. By eating it, I was focused on what I was eating. I was eating life. I was feeding myself on life.

I wasn't just meditating on his suffering but was now meditating on eating resurrection life! This was not the body of death but the body of life. I took several bites and chewed slowly, allowing the reality of His life in the bread to flood all through me. I found myself in an amazing intimacy with Jesus that I had never experienced before in Communion.

He then repeated the process with me when I took the cup. It could no longer be a small sip, as that is not drinking. He said to drink it, which requires more than a tablespoon of juice. He led me through the same process. He wanted me to have enough juice to take multiple drinks while meditating on the power of the blood of Jesus and, more importantly, remember it is the Cup of the New Testament in His blood.

Before this happened, I had become very dissatisfied with the prepackaged Communion cups. While they were convenient, they were hard to open, and the little piece of bread was not enough to chew. The cup had a tablespoon of juice that was barely enough to swallow. I didn't like using them personally, and I thought we had cheapened the Lord's Table in Communion, especially in our services. This issue became very real to me in a Pastors and leaders gathering for Communion and prayer.

I struggled to open the bread, and finally, I removed the bread and opened the cup of juice. With the pastor leading us to take the bread, I soon realized the prepackaged cups needed to end.

The bread was a round nickel-sized piece as thin as paper. I put it in my mouth, and it dissolved like a Listerine breath strip. I almost laughed aloud at the thought, realized the total emptiness in the prepackaged cups, and said no more.

God is calling us to a Communion Reformation in the church and our personal lives. We must no longer make Communion CONVENIENT with tiny plastic cups but one that honors the Sacredness of the bread and cup. Let's return the Holy to the Lord's Sacred Communion.

They Knew Him In The Breaking Of Bread

Another Scripture in Luke 24 is about two disciples on the Road to Emmaus. It is incredibly revealing about the benefits of breaking bread with Jesus and what happens when we do.

> *30 Now it came to pass, as He sat at the table with them, that He took bread, blessed and broke it, and gave it to them. 31 <u>Then their eyes were opened, and they knew Him</u>, and He vanished from their sight.* – Luke 24:30-31 NKJV

Days earlier, they had Passover with Jesus, and He did the same thing then as He did this day. He took the bread, blessed it, broke it, and gave it to them. Immediately, their eyes were opened, and they KNEW HIM! They knew Him in the breaking of bread. This can be the same for us today if we slow down and take the time with Him in Communion.

> *32 And they said to one another, "Did not our heart burn within us while He talked with us on the road, and while He opened the Scriptures to us?" 33 So they rose up that very hour and returned to Jerusalem and found the eleven and those who were with them gathered together, 34 saying, "The Lord is risen indeed, and has appeared to Simon!"*
>
> *35 And they told about the things that had happened on the road, and <u>how He was known to them in the breaking of bread</u>.* Luke 24:32-35

It is no wonder they broke bread from house to house

every day in Acts. When you partake of the bread again, slow down and get to know Him in that moment. I continue to come closer to Him and find greater intimacy with Him when I do. His presence and the essence of His glory are now more real to me during Communion, and I carry His presence throughout the day. It can be the same for you.

Slow down and enjoy Him!

Chapter 6

Key Words & Phrases

As I lay on the floor in prayer, preparing for Communion, I found myself captivated by the verses in I Corinthians 11:23-25. The Lord's presence was all-encompassing, and time seemed to slow as He directed my attention to specific words in these verses. I would fixate on each word, meditating on its meaning while soaking in His presence.

I was filled with a sense of awe and reverence, knowing that I should not move on to the next word until He guided me. As I prayed in the Spirit, revelation was poured into me, bringing a profound understanding. I was struck by the awe-inspiring nature of what I saw and understood in each word.

I cannot overstate the transformative power of understanding the deeper meanings of these words and how they are used in relation to Holy Communion. This understanding will enrich your personal Communion time and empower you to experience the depth of Communion in church services.

These are the keywords that carry significant weight in our Communion experience. Each of these words or phrases, are not just words, but they hold the key to a deeper and more impactful encounter with Jesus during Communion.

- Took
- Broke (broken)
- Eat
- Thanks
- Cup of the new covenant in My Blood
- As often
- Remembrance
- Proclaim
- Come

We must go beyond just reading these verses, eating the bread, drinking the cup, and saying we have had Communion. That experience is limited, and shallow compared to what is genuinely in Communion and what the Lord has made available to us. Each of these words carries great significance for our understanding and the true and deep experience we can have in Communion with Jesus. We should encounter Him every time. Let's look at them.

> *[23] For I received from the Lord that which I also delivered to you: that the Lord Jesus on the same night in which He was betrayed* ***took*** *bread; [24] and when He had given* ***thanks***, *He* ***broke*** *it and said, "Take,* ***eat***; *this is My body which is* ***broken*** *for you; do this in* ***remembrance*** *of Me." [25] In the same*

*manner, He also took the cup after supper, saying, "This **cup is the new covenant in My blood**. This do, **as often** as you drink it, in **remembrance** of Me. For **as often** as you eat the bread and drink this cup, you proclaim the Lord's death till He comes.* - I Corinthians 11:23-26 NKJV

He Gave Thanks

In previous chapters, we have looked at the words *took, broke, eat, and drink. Thanks,* is the next focus word. After Jesus took the middle piece of bread from the matzoh tosh, He gave thanks before breaking it. This revelation was so simple, profound, and deep that it overwhelmed me. With tears running down my face, my heart was full of gratitude for what He had done for me and how He was showing Himself to me in such Holiness. All I could think about was giving Him thanks and worshiping Him while lying prone on the floor in my dark prayer closet.

My thanksgiving rolled into worship, and then the Scriptures rolled through me like a wave. We are to offer God our thanksgiving and magnify Him with thanksgiving. We come into His presence with thanksgiving and enter into His courts with thanksgiving. We offer the sacrifice of thanksgiving and sing with thanksgiving.

Communion Encounters

He was teaching me how to have Holy Communion in a place of Holiness and Sacredness. Sitting next to me was a cup of juice and the matzo bread, but I knew I should not touch either one. He was showing me that coming from a place of a heart filled with gratitude is how I was to start having Communion going forward and that I must teach others this truth.

Communion should always start with expressing our heartfelt thanksgiving to the Father, Son, and Holy Spirit. We must be willing to take our time. God is calling church leaders to return Communion to a place of Holiness and Sacredness in their services and give the people time to enter His presence with thanksgiving, not just dwell on His sufferings and death. He was raised from the dead!

We must stop looking at the clock and allow the Holy Spirit to work in the hearts of God's people. If it takes thirty minutes or longer, the results will speak for themselves, and no one will be disappointed.

I now find Communion in church services lacking and incomplete for every believer participating. Let's make the reforms, allow the people to encounter Jesus during Communion, and end Communion with a celebration of song and praise.

I keep telling people that when I follow the process He gave me that morning, I can spend thirty to sixty minutes in Communion before I start praying about anything. It is a personal and intimate time with Jesus, and I am not in a hurry. Thanksgiving prepares the heart, and your experience of His presence will be greatly enhanced as you enjoy the bread and the cup of life from a place of gratitude.

There are many Scriptures about thanksgiving, and I am providing some that you can incorporate into your Communion time and utilize in personal and prayerful decrees.

> *Sing praise to the Lord, you saints of His, And give thanks at the remembrance of His holy name.* - Psalm 30:4 NKJV

> *I will give You thanks in the great assembly; I will praise You among many people.* - Psalm 35:18 NKJV

> *We give thanks to You, O God, we give thanks! For Your wondrous works declare that Your name is near.* - Psalm 75:1 NKJV

> *It is good to give thanks to the Lord, and to sing praises to Your name, O Most High;* [2] *To declare Your lovingkindness in the morning, and Your faithfulness every night.* - Psalm 92:1-2 KNJV

Let us come before His presence with thanksgiving; Let us shout joyfully to Him with psalms. - Psalm 95:2 NKJV

But we thank God for giving us the victory as conquerors through our Lord Jesus, the Anointed One. - I Corinthians 15:57, The Passion Translation

Now thanks be to God who always leads us in triumph in Christ, and through us diffuses the fragrance of His knowledge in every place. - II Corinthians 2:24 NKJV

Thanks be to God for His indescribable gift! - II Corinthians 9:15 NKJV

We give You thanks, O Lord God Almighty, The One who is and who was and who is to come because You have taken Your great power and reigned. - Revelation 11:17 NKJV

As Often

Twice, Jesus said, *"As often,"* as a simple reminder that He gave no specific instructions or guidance concerning how often or when we should have Communion.

The Passover He was sharing had a set time, but He was introducing the New Covenant and new ways. I have heard people say we should have it every Sunday morning, and others say once a month is appropriate. Stop the debate and go with what Jesus said. *As often as you do this.*

I know people who have Communion daily and sometimes multiple times. I have it often and for various reasons. During my devotional times and when I am deeply praying for others, I see the act of taking Communion as a spiritual weapon and to make a decree.

When we take Communion, I believe it has significant spiritual consequences that impact our everyday lives. Communion is active participation in the covenant with the Father, Son, and Holy Spirit, and all three actively participate.

When I am hungry for more of His presence, I know I will find it during Communion. In those times, I find myself in special times of unplanned prayer that becomes very focused as the Holy Spirit leads me to pray more specifically.

How awesome is our God that we can be so intimate with Him that he tells us whom and what to pray for, knowing He wants to answer that prayer?

While there can be many reasons for having Communion, the most essential point is to do it as often as you like, and more is better. Start by setting a few times in the week for Communion. It can be in your private devotions, with your spouse, family, or a friend. How often you do, is your individual choice.

If I ever pastor a church again, I know we would combine Communion into our praise and worship in the Sunday morning service and not put a time limit on it.

Communion is a special time for believers, and leaders must refuse the traditions and time limits and allow the Holy Spirit to touch and change hearts during that time.

It would also make the praise and worship more meaningful. Remember the fourth cup of praise in Passover? They sang hymns from Psalms 113 through 118. Communion should end with a joyful celebration, not a hushed mood of solemnity.

Remembrance

Twice, when Jesus told us to eat the bread and again when He told us to drink the cup, He said, *"do this in remembrance of Me."*

What is it like when you have communion at church? What do you remember, and what do you meditate on? It is probably the same for you when you have personal Communion. It's what we have been programmed to think about.

We are led to remember and place our focus and meditation on His sufferings and death. We were lost in sin, and He was the Lamb of God who suffered and died so we would not perish into eternal hell but be born again and receive the gift of eternal life and be saved.

But was His death the end of it? What else could we remember? My wife and I have discussed this for years and always believed people were missing out on what God wants us to experience in Communion. Even in recent years, we would leave a church service that had ended with Communion and when the people left, it looked like they were leaving a funeral home.

Why are people seemingly so gloomy after Communion? Something was missing in the experience. The focus is only on His suffering and death, which must change. We need to remember the whole picture!

Remember It All – And Proclaim It!

When I was meditating on the word "remember," the Holy Spirit kept showing me the bigger picture of remembrance, and it revolutionized how I receive and enjoy Communion now. Here are the six things He gave me that morning.

He showed me to remember and acknowledge the pre-eminence of Jesus.

> *In the beginning was the Word, and the Word was with God, and the Word was God.* [2] *He was in the beginning with God.* [3] *All things were made through Him, and without Him, nothing was made that was made.* [4] *In Him was life, and the life was the light of men.*
>
> [14] *And the Word became flesh and dwelt among us, and we beheld His glory, the glory as of the only begotten of the Father, full of grace and truth.* - John 1:1-4, 14 NKJV

He showed me to remember and acknowledge the sufferings and death of Jesus.

> *Surely, He has borne our griefs and carried our sorrows; yet we esteemed Him stricken, Smitten by God, and afflicted.* [5] *But He was wounded for our transgressions, He was bruised for our iniquities; The chastisement for our peace was upon Him, And by His stripes, we are healed.* - Isaiah 53:4-5 (Also Isaiah 53:1-12; Psalm 22:1-21) NKJV

He showed me to remember and acknowledge the resurrection of Jesus.

> *Until the day in which He was taken up, after He through the Holy Spirit had given commandments to the apostles whom He had chosen, ³ to whom He also presented Himself alive after His suffering by many infallible proofs, being seen by them during forty days and speaking of the things pertaining to the kingdom of God.* - Acts 1:2-3 (Also Matthew 28:5-7) NKJV

He showed me to remember and acknowledge the ascension of Jesus.

> *And He led them out as far as Bethany, and He lifted up His hands and blessed them. ⁵¹Now it came to pass, while He blessed them, that He was parted from them and carried up into heaven. ⁵² And they worshiped Him and returned to Jerusalem with great joy, ⁵³ and were continually in the temple praising and blessing God. Amen.* - Luke 24:50-53 NKJV

> *Now when He had spoken these things, while they watched, He was taken up, and a cloud received Him out of their sight.* - Acts 1:9 NKJV

He showed me to remember and acknowledge the soon and coming return of Jesus.

> *And while they looked steadfastly toward heaven as He went up, behold, two men stood by them in white apparel, ¹¹ who also said, "Men of Galilee, why do you stand gazing up into heaven? This same Jesus, who was taken up from you into heaven, will so come in like manner as you saw Him go into heaven." -* Acts 1:10-11 NKJV

> *For the Lord Himself will descend from heaven with a shout, with the voice of an archangel, and with the trumpet of God. And the dead in Christ will rise first. ¹⁷ Then we who are alive and remain shall be caught up together with them in the clouds to meet the Lord in the air. And thus, we shall always be with the Lord. -* I Thessalonians 4:16-17 NKJV

He showed me to remember and acknowledge that I will spend eternity with Jesus in His Glory!

> *For God so loved the world that He gave His only begotten Son, that whoever believes in Him should not perish but have everlasting life. -* John 3:16 NKJV

A Time Of Awakening

Most assuredly, I say to you, he who believes in Me has everlasting life. - John 6:47 NKJV

If you confess with your mouth the Lord Jesus and believe in your heart that God has raised Him from the dead, you will be saved. [10] For with the heart one believes unto righteousness, and with the mouth, confession is made unto salvation. - Romans 10:9-10 KNJV

For each of these six areas of remembrance, there are many Scriptures to strengthen us during Communion. The process of Communion the Lord has shown me and that I am laying out to you in this book is easily implemented in our personal Communion times. It just means we will no longer treat Communion like we are going through a fast-food drive-through.

However, it will require a major reformation in the churches, and the leaders will need a fresh revelation of the encountering power of Communion for their congregations.

It will be a challenge because the traditions of men that have been handed down still make the Word of God of no effect today, just as it did in Mark 7:13.

The congregations embracing the change will

experience the Lord in new and wonderful ways during Communion. They should expect to see salvations, prodigals return to Christ, healings, miracles, and bondages broken in people's lives. I am praying for you!

How hungry are you for His presence and awakening? Are you willing to see a reformation of Communion in your church?

Proclaim

This is the last word He gave me to focus on, and what He tied together is very important.

> *For as often as you eat the bread and drink this cup, you proclaim the Lord's death till He comes.* - I Corinthians 11:26 NKJV

The Lord tied two words together and made a strong point of emphasis. He took the word remembrance and connected it to "proclaim." The word is connected to proclaiming the Lord's death, but there is not a period after the word death, and yet, that's how many treat it. We are too singularly focused on His suffering and death to notice the sentence has a continuation of thought. We proclaim His death till he COMES.

He had to be raised from the dead to come back to

life, and He was resurrected. We need to appreciate the fullness of thought in this verse during Communion. We must and can proclaim His coming because He was raised from the dead. That is our proclamation, and we should shout it from the rooftops! We are proclaiming His death, burial, and resurrection until He comes again.

When we eat the bread and drink the cup, we should remember the six things we have reviewed and apply them to Communion. As often as we do this, we proclaim these truths until He comes. The focus is not on death but on resurrection life!

Communion Encounters

Chapter 7

The Blood Covenant

At the end of the Passover meal, Jesus picked up the third cup, the Cup of Redemption, and made an amazing declaration. Jesus spoke six powerful and life-changing words!

> *In the same manner, He also took the cup after supper, saying, "This cup is the new covenant in My blood. This do, as often as you drink it, in remembrance of Me."* - I Corinthians 11:25 NKJV

We have read this verse and heard it many times in services during Communion. This was another phrase the Lord had me meditate on, and He had a particular point to make. What's in the blood?

We know from Leviticus 17:11, that *the life of the flesh is in the blood,* and again in verse 14, *for it is the life of all flesh. Its blood sustains its life.* Life is in the blood, and this is well-known among believers. Our atonement is in the blood, and we are cleansed of our sins by the shed blood of Jesus. But He wanted me to see more than that.

He directed my focus to the phrase "new covenant in" and it became abundantly clear. Yes, life is in the blood, but through the blood, the entire new covenant and all its blessings and promises are available to us! Every time we drink the cup, we are personally partaking in the new covenant's blessings and promises and the life it contains. Jesus made this very clear in the following verse in the book of John.

> Then Jesus said to them, *"Most assuredly, I say to you, unless you eat the flesh of the Son of Man and drink His blood, you have no life in you. [54] Whoever eats My flesh and drinks My blood has eternal life, and I will raise him up at the last day.* - John 6:53-54 NKJV

If we better understand the Covenant, we can more effectively claim, decree, receive, and experience the fullness of the new covenant's blessings as often as we continue to drink its cup.

The Significance of Communion's Covenant Is The Blood

Without blood, there is no remission of sin. His blood cleanses us from sin *rather than covering* our sins, as in the Old Covenant. After the blood cleanses us, the blood claims us. We are bought at a price, and we are no longer our own. Jesus bought us, cleansed us, and claimed us as His own. This is a significant revelation that all of Christ's followers should celebrate in every Communion we have.

A Time Of Awakening

For this is My blood of the new covenant, which is shed for many for the remission of sins. - Matthew 26:28 NKJV

The Passover celebration was the last meal Jesus shared with the Apostles before His death, and it was there that He chose to transform the meaning of both the bread and cup into the reality of a New Covenant. Through Jesus as the Lamb of God, a new and living way into God's presence and provision was being prepared.

The First Sacrifice and Shedding of Blood

Also, for Adam and his wife, the Lord God made tunics of skin and clothed them. - Genesis 3:21 NKJV

God was the first to sacrifice and shed the blood of an animal to cover sin, as He did for Adam and Eve. God was also the last to offer a sacrifice for sin when He gave His only Son to be the Lamb of God. The first time, He provided a covering for sin for Adam and Eve, and the last time, with Jesus, He provided cleansing of sin with the blood of Jesus and a New Covenant built on better promises.

Without the shedding of blood, there is no remission of sin. - Hebrews 9:22 NKJV

Remission means a release from bondage or imprisonment, forgiveness or pardon, or a remission of the penalty. That is why we say the blood of Jesus sets us free!

When God sacrificed the innocent animal for Adam and Eve, He was declaring the only way to have fellowship with Him was through the shedding of blood. The covenant God established required innocent animals to be sacrificed to provide a covering for the guilty. The principle of exchanging a life for a life was established. But it was still only a covering and not a cleansing of sin.

As Scripture tells us, Jesus, being innocent, fulfilled this requirement as the Lamb of God. Jesus was the innocent sacrifice.

> *He (Jesus) who knew no sin was made sin for us so we might be made the righteousness of God in Him.* - II Corinthians 5:21 NKJV

Cain & Abel

Adam told both of his sons about the sacrifice of an innocent animal, the shedding of blood, and the need to bring an offering to God as part of the Adamic Covenant. We see in these verses that Cain rejected the blood covenant and brought an offering of the fruit of the ground to the Lord.

A Time Of Awakening

Abel understood that God would only accept him through the shed blood of the firstborn lamb of his flock. God respected Abel's offering but did not respect Cain's offering, which caused Cain to become very angry.

> *And in the process of time, it came to pass that Cain brought an offering of the fruit of the ground to the LORD. [4] Abel also brought of the firstborn of his flock and of their fat. And the LORD respected Abel and his offering, [5] but He did not respect Cain and his offering. And Cain was very angry, and his countenance fell.*
>
> *[6] So the LORD said to Cain, "Why are you angry? And why has your countenance fallen? [7] If you do well, will you not be accepted? And if you do not do well, sin lies at the door. And its desire is for you, but you should rule over it."*
>
> *[8] Now Cain talked with Abel, his brother, and it came to pass, when they were in the field, that Cain rose up against Abel, his brother, and killed him. [9] Then the LORD said to Cain, "Where is Abel your brother?" [10] And He said, "What have you done? The voice of your brother's blood cries out to Me from the ground.* - Genesis 4:3-10 NKJV

The Blood Proves Essential For Right Standing With God

The issue of blood sacrifice as being essential for a right standing with God is conveyed through the offerings of Cain and Abel. Pursuant upon the founding lesson God gave in dealing with Adam and Eve's sin, Cain's vegetable offering, the fruit of his own efforts, was an offering of self-righteous refusal to live under God's revealed covenant.

Adam's attempt to use fig leaves for covering was rejected, and so was Cain's offering, but Abel's offering of a blood sacrifice was pleasing to God. God's sacrifice of animals in the Garden established the blood sacrifice necessary for approaching Him. Right standing before a covenant-making God was shown to be a matter of life and death, not merely a matter of one's good efforts. From Kingdom Dynamics, NKJV

Cain rejected the blood covenant, and Abel understood it by faith and is mentioned in the Faith Hall of Fame in Hebrews 11.

> *By faith, Abel offered to God a more excellent sacrifice than Cain, through which he obtained witness that he was righteous, God testifying of his gifts; and through it, he being dead still speaks.* - Hebrews 11:4 NKJV

Without the blood, no one can have God's favor, fellowship with Him, obtain His blessings and promises, or approach Him.

Noah's First Act After The Flood

When the Lord told Noah to gather the animals, He told him to take seven each of every clean animal, a male and his female, and two each of the unclean animals, and seven each of birds, both male and female, to keep the species alive on the face of the earth. Remember, only "clean" animals could be used in a sacrifice to God. (Genesis 7:1-3)

Once the water had descended, the Lord told them to leave the ark and bring out the animals. After leaving the ark and standing on the ground again, Noah's first act was to immediately build an altar and sacrifice the clean animals.

God had passed judgment on the earth, and Noah was now baptizing the earth with the blood of the sacrifice, which brought back God's favor and blessings. The Lord had not directed Noah to offer a sacrifice, but Noah did it to show God his gratitude for their deliverance. Noah's sacrifice was pleasing to the Lord, and in response, the Lord made a covenant not to destroy creation with a flood again, and it was established by blood.

Then Noah built an altar to the Lord, and took of every clean animal and of every clean bird, and offered burnt offerings on the altar. [21] And the Lord smelled a soothing aroma. Then the Lord said in His heart, "I will never again curse the ground for man's sake, although the imagination of man's heart is evil from his youth; nor will I again destroy every living thing as I have done. [22] "While the earth remains, seedtime and harvest, cold and heat, winter and summer, and day and night shall not cease." - Genesis 8:20-22 NKJV

There is no direct command instructing Noah to make this blood sacrifice, suggesting this practice had been established and handed down from Adam.

This is the first time in biblical history we see the term "covenant" applied to the relationship between God and an individual and their descendants, and it was established in blood. (Genesis 9:1-17)

And as for Me, behold, I establish My covenant with you and with your descendants after you. - Genesis 9:9 NKJV

Thus, I establish My covenant with you: Never again shall all flesh be cut off by the waters of the flood; never again shall there

be a flood to destroy the earth." - Genesis 9:11 NKJV

And God said: "This is the sign of the covenant which I make between Me and you, and every living creature that is with you, for perpetual generations. - Genesis 9:12 NKJV

And God said to Noah, "This is the sign of the covenant which I have established between Me and all flesh that is on the earth." - Genesis 9:17 NKJV

Abram Builds An Altar

Genesis chapters 12 through 14 are powerful stories that are a stepping-stone for Abram into the blood covenant, which is established in Genesis 15 and carries over to us through the redemptive work of Jesus Christ. There are some key areas for us to look at regarding the Abrahamic Covenant.

Now the Lord had said to Abram: "Get out of your country, from your family and from your father's house, to a land that I will show you. ² I will make you a great nation; I will bless you and make your name great, and you shall be a blessing. ³ I will bless those who bless you, and I will curse him who curses you, and in you all the families of the earth shall

> *be blessed." ⁷ Then the Lord appeared to Abram and said, "To your descendants, I will give this land." And there he built an altar to the Lord, who had appeared to him.* - Genesis 12:1-3, 7 NKJV

After directing Abram to depart his own country, the Lord declared His promises to him. Departing his country, Abram journeyed into Canan, which was part of the promised land. Once there, the Lord appeared to him and declared He was giving this land to Abram's descendants.

Abrams's response to this promise is significant. In verse 7, it says he built an altar to the Lord. If he built an altar, it was for offering a sacrifice involving the shedding of blood. *Without the blood, the promise would never happen. The blood brought the promise!*

This is important. When we take the bread and cup in Communion, we are participating in and activating all that is promised in the covenant that is in and through the blood of Jesus. Knowing the Scriptures of the New Testament (Covenant) allows us to knowingly and intentionally declare in faith all the promises it contains for our lives.

Abram and Melchizedek

Because the land could not support both Lot and

Abram and to avoid strife between their herdsmen, they decided to separate and go in different directions. Lot chose the plain of Jordan, leaving the land of Canaan for Abram. In time, Lot was captured in a war between kings, including the King of Sodom. Upon learning Lot had been captured, Abram armed his trained servants and attacked Lot's captors.

Victorious in the battle, Abram brought back all the goods that had been taken, rescuing Lot and his goods, the women, and all the people taken captive. Upon his return, the king of Sodom went out to meet Abram. Also coming out to meet Abram was Melchizedek.

Who was Melchizedek? His name means "My King is Righteous," but there is more.

> *For this Melchizedek, king of Salem, priest of the Most High God, who met Abraham returning from the slaughter of the kings and blessed him, ² to whom also Abraham gave a tenth part of all, first being translated "king of righteousness," and then also king of Salem, meaning "king of peace," ³ without father, without mother, without genealogy, having neither beginning of days nor end of life, but made like the Son of God, remains a priest continually.* - Hebrews 7:1-3 NKJV

Melchizedek was the king of Salem, and Salem means peace and was also the early name for Jerusalem. He was the king of Peace. Most Jewish commentators also affirm that Salem is the same place as Jerusalem. In Isaiah 9:6, Jesus is called the Prince of Peace.

Melchizedek is also called the priest of God Most High. Jesus is called a high priest forever after the order of Melchizedek in Hebrews 5:5-6, and again in verse 10, *"called of God a high priest after the order of Melchizedek."*

Jesus fulfilled the requirements of the priesthood and was appointed by God rather than man.

He experienced true humanity and made a one-time sacrifice for sin when He offered Himself as the Lamb of God who would take away the sins of the world.

Abram's encounter with Melchizedek was an encounter with the antitype of Jesus in His role as our High Priest. Jesus said as much in John 8:56, *"Your father Abraham rejoiced to see My day, and he saw it and was glad."*

The Two Offers

When Melchizedek came out to meet Abram, he

offered him bread and wine. The king of Sodom also presented an offer of all the goods and spoils taken in battle. But Abram chose only one.

> *And the king of Sodom went out to meet him at the Valley of Shaveh (that is, the King's Valley) after his return from the defeat of Chedorlaomer and the kings who were with him.* - Genesis 14:17 NKJV

> *18 Then Melchizedek, king of Salem, brought out bread and wine; he was the priest of God Most High. 19 And he blessed him and said: "Blessed be Abram of God Most High, Possessor of heaven and earth; 20 and blessed be God Most High, who has delivered your enemies into your hand." and he gave him a tithe of all.* - Genesis 14:18-20 NKJV

> *21 Now the king of Sodom said to Abram, "Give me the persons, and take the goods for yourself."* - Genesis 14:21 NKJV

His choice was the bread and the wine, and the King of Salem, who was also a priest of the most High God, announced a blessing upon Abram as a result in celebration of his victory in battle. Seeing this take place, the King of Sodom offered Abram all of the goods taken in battle, and Abrams's response shows his heart after God.

> *But Abram said to the king of Sodom, "I have raised my hand to the Lord, God Most High, the Possessor of heaven and earth, [23] that I will take nothing, from a thread to a sandal strap, and that I will not take anything that is yours, lest you should say, 'I have made Abram rich.'"* - Genesis 14:22-23 NKJV

While there is no indication that the bread and wine offered by Melchizedek are related to the bread and cup of the new covenant offered by Jesus, there are a couple of key takeaways.

The priest of the Most-High God offered Abram something special with the bread and wine. He was also offered the things of this world. Abram refused the worldly spoils of battle and showed his true heart to walk with and be pleasing to the Most-High God he knew. He was going to walk in Covenant with God, who had already made Abram rich.

Jesus is the eternal King and High Priest. He is the King of righteousness and the King of Peace, and like Melchizedek, he offers us the bread and the cup of the New Covenant in His blood.

Chapter 8

The Abrahamic Covenant

In Genesis 15, the Lord responded to Abram's choice to accept bread and wine from Melchizedek instead of the spoils of battle. The Lord renewed His previous promises to Abram and established the first direct requirement of a blood sacrifice to establish a covenant, which is directly related to Jesus establishing the New Covenant in His blood, which we celebrate in Communion.

This chapter further leads to the establishment of the Abrahamic Covenant in Genesis 17, which has significant meaning to us.

As you will see, having a basic understanding of the Abrahamic Covenant will significantly benefit you and enhance your experience with the Lord in Communion.

When the Lord spoke to Abram in a vision in Genesis 15, Abram brought up the reality that he still had no offspring. He sought to reckon his childlessness with the past promise and did so with understanding and a proper heart. In response, the Lord made two declarations to Abram at that time.

First, the Lord lovingly told Abram not to be afraid,

for He is his shield and an exceedingly great reward for Abrams's heir would come from his own body. To encourage and build Abram's confidence, the Lord shows him the heavens and stars and says, "So *shall your descendants be."* And Abram believed in the Lord and God accounted it to him for righteousness. - Genesis 15:6 NKJV

Then, the Lord tells him that He is giving him land as his inheritance, a promise that fills Abram with hope and expectation. When Abram asks how he would know this, the Lord gives a tremendous response. The Lord sets up the first requirement of a blood sacrifice to establish a covenant. God is setting the stage for a "covenant-cutting" ceremony, where covenants are established in blood.

The Stage Is Set

> *Then He said to him, "I am the Lord, who brought you out of Ur of the Chaldeans, to give you this land to inherit it."* *8 And he said, "Lord God, how shall I know that I will inherit it?"*
>
> *9 So He said to him, "Bring Me a three-year-old heifer, a three-year-old female goat, a three-year-old ram, a turtledove, and a young pigeon."*

A Time Of Awakening

[10] Then he brought all these to Him and cut them in two, down the middle, and placed each piece opposite the other; but he did not cut the birds in two. - Genesis 15:7-10 NKJV

The term "cut covenant" comes from this ceremony, and in verse 18, which says, *"the Lord made a covenant,"* but in Hebrew, it says "cut" covenant.

The animals to be offered were selected, then cut into halves and arranged in proper order opposite each other, with a separation between them, which allowed the people to walk between the two sides. The covenant parties then walked between the halves, indicating they were irrevocably bound together in a blood covenant.

How the animals were prepared relates to Jesus, who was pierced, cut with the stripes on His back, and who shed His blood on the ground as the Lamb of God sacrificed for the sins of the world and who is the Mediator of a better (new) covenant that was established on better promises. (Hebrews 8:6)

The shedding of innocent lifeblood confirmed the sacred nature of this covenant bond. But the Lord does something of great significance in accepting the sacrifice.

Only God passed between the pieces, indicating that

it was His covenant and that He alone would assume total responsibility for administering the covenant and its promises.

On that day, God walked alone to establish a covenant made from the shed blood of innocent life, and I see a direct correlation with Jesus. Jesus walked alone to Calvary to establish the New Covenant in His blood. He, too, would take on the sole responsibility of performing the responsibilities of the New Covenant in His blood with those who would accept Him.

> *And it came to pass when the sun went down, and it was dark, that behold, there appeared a smoking oven and a burning torch that passed between those pieces.*
>
> *[18] On the same day the Lord made a covenant with Abram, saying: "To your descendants, I have given this land, from the river of Egypt to the great river, the River Euphrates [19] the Kenites, the Kenezzites, the Kadmonites, [20] the Hittites, the Perizzites, the Rephaim, [21] the Amorites, the Canaanites, the Girgashites, and the Jebusites."* - Genesis 15:17-21 NKJV

The smoking oven and burning torch are metaphors for one single blazing fire. In this case, it is the

Shekinah glory and presence of the Lord Himself who passed between the pieces.

God's oath was unconditional, and He placed no demands on Abram to participate in the covenant. Significantly, God walked alone between the bleeding pieces of animals, an act of loyalty to the covenant, and Abram, his covenant partner. This also set the stage for Jesus and a New Covenant in His blood.

God required nothing from Abram to establish the covenant relationship that day. In the New Covenant, Jesus only requires repentance of sin and a confession of our faith in His death, burial, and resurrection that Jesus is Lord. We are saved by grace through faith and not by *works*.

There are three critical components in this covenant. First, the bond originated from God's initiative. Second, offering a blood sacrifice was required for the covenant to exist. Third, God took sole ownership of ensuring the outcome of His oath in the covenant. This would also hold true for the New Covenant, except that God would be the one to offer His Lamb for the sacrifice.

Thirteen Years Later – The Abrahamic Covenant

Thirteen years later, when Abram was 99 years old,

the Lord appeared to Abram again and set in motion the Abrahamic Covenant.

I suggest you read the entire chapter of Genesis 17, as it is rich in revelation and is one of the most important chapters in the Bible because it describes in detail the establishment of the Abrahamic covenant, which would eventually be fulfilled in Jesus Christ.

The first thing the Lord does when appearing to Abram is to declare and remind him who He is, followed by the declaration that He is making a covenant with him.

> *When Abram was ninety-nine years old, the Lord appeared to Abram and said to him, "I am Almighty God; walk before Me and be blameless. ² And I will make My covenant between Me and you and will multiply you exceedingly."* - Genesis 17:1-2 NKJV

The Hebrew name for Almighty God is *El Shaddai*. It means mighty, unconquerable, most powerful, and all-sufficient God, eternally capable of being all His people need.

He then tells Abram that He is making a covenant between them and will multiply Abram exceedingly.

A Time Of Awakening

When the all-sufficient God, who is unconquerable, tells you He will do something, be like Abram and take Him at His word. He is an exceedingly great God, and we call Him Father!

God Changes Abram's Name

> *No longer shall your name be called Abram, but your name shall be Abraham, for I have made you a father of many nations.* - Genesis 17:5 NKJV

The Bible teaches us that words are important, and faith calls those things that do not exist as if they did. (Romans 4:17) God changed Abram's name to Abraham based on His covenant promise that he would become the father of many nations. God saw the covenant in full effect and Abraham as a father. Abraham means "Father of a Multitude."

In the future, every time Abraham heard or spoke his name, he would remember God's promise and would declare the promise of God that he was the Father of many nations. Abraham embraced the covenant promise in full faith that God would fulfill His promise.

> *He did not waver at the promise of God through unbelief but was strengthened in Faith giving Glory to God and being fully*

convinced that what He had promised He was also able to perform. - Romans 4:20-21 NKJV

God made it clear that He would establish an everlasting covenant with Abraham. A covenant is a pledge, contract, or agreement, and here, the Lord makes an irrevocable pledge to Abraham and his descendants forever.

> *And I will establish My covenant between Me and you and your descendants after you in their generations, for an everlasting covenant, to be God to you and your descendants after you.* - Genesis 17:7 NKJV

Sign Of The Covenant

God finally makes a demand on Abraham as His covenant partner and for Abraham's descendants. Circumcision was an external sign that Abraham and his descendants were to execute to show they were God's covenant people. It expressed confidence in God's covenant promises and faithfulness rather than in their own fleshly dependence.

> *This is My covenant which you shall keep, between Me and you and your descendants after you: Every male child among you shall be circumcised; [11] and you shall be*

*circumcised in the flesh of your foreskins,
and it shall be a sign of the covenant between
Me and you.* - Genesis 17:10-11 NKJV

Sarai Gets A Name Change

Sarai was also brought into this covenant, and God changed her name to Sarah. God promised to bless her and give Abraham a son by her, making her the mother of nations and kings. Abraham thought this was so funny that he fell on his face and laughed. He questioned how a one-hundred-year-old man and ninety-year-old woman could bear a child, and they both laughed in unbelief.

But God's unrelenting response was that she would bear a son and call him Isaac. Moreover, God declares He will establish His covenant with Isaac for an everlasting covenant and with his descendants. God tells them she will bear Isaac next year at the set time. When God finished talking with him, the Bible says God went up from Abraham, which is a fantastic thought. One year later, Isaac, the child of promise, was born.

The Lord Confirms Covenant With Isaac

Isaac was born when Abraham was 100 years old, and Genesis 25 tells us that Abraham lived to be 175 years old. The Lord then instructs Isaac not to go to

Egypt but to live in the land the Lord would show him. He confirms that He will uphold the covenant with Abraham.

> *Dwell in this land, and I will be with you and bless you, for to you and your descendants I give all these lands, and I will perform the oath which I swore to Abraham your father.* - Genesis 26:3 NKJV

The Lord is the God who keeps His covenant and has mercy on the servants who walk before Him with all their hearts. The Lord declared He would perform His solemn oath with Abraham and assured Isaac he would have numberless descendants for Abraham's sake. He then appeared to Isaac and clearly stated He would multiply Isaac's descendants, which led Isaac to build an altar. All of this leads to Jesus as the seed of Abraham and the New Covenant.

> *And the Lord appeared to him the same night and said, "I am the God of your father, Abraham; do not fear, for I am with you. I will bless you and multiply your descendants for My servant Abraham's sake."* [25] *So he built an altar there and called on the name of the Lord, and he pitched his tent there, and there Isaac's servants dug a well.* - Genesis 26:24-25 NKJV

After the Lord appeared to him and confirmed his oath to uphold the covenant, Isaac built an altar for a sacrifice and shedding of innocent lifeblood. Isaac understood its significance and called on the name of the Lord at the altar.

Jesus - The Promised Seed Of Abraham

Jesus said, *"This is the cup of the new covenant in My blood."*

We must not lose focus on why understanding the progression of the various covenants is so essential. They bring us to Jesus and show us what He has done for us as Abraham's seed. They lead us into a covenant relationship with Almighty God through the blood of Jesus and make us knowledgeable partakers of the covenant.

> *Now to Abraham and his Seed were the promises made. He does not say, "And to seeds," as of many, but as of one, "And to your Seed," who is Christ.* - Galatians 3:16 NKJV

You Are An Heir Of Abraham Through Jesus

> *For you are all sons of God through faith in Christ Jesus. [27] For as many of you as were baptized into Christ have put on*

Christ. [28] There is neither Jew nor Greek, there is neither slave nor free, there is neither male nor female; for you are all one in Christ Jesus.

[29] And if you are Christ's, then you are Abraham's seed, and heirs according to the promise. - Galatians 3:26-29 NKJV

You are what God's word says you are. You are an heir according to God's promise in the Abrahamic Covenant. Lay hold of this truth the next time you lift the cup of the New Covenant in His blood to your mouth.

What is it that you are laying hold of? The promises are yours and you need to press into them in faith. Drink it in faith and receive the promises of God in Christ!

You Are The Redeemed For A Purpose

Christ has redeemed us from the curse of the law, having become a curse for us (for it is written, "Cursed is everyone who hangs on a tree"), [14] that the blessing of Abraham might come upon the Gentiles in Christ Jesus, that we might receive the promise of the Spirit through faith. - Galatians 3:13-14 NKJV

A Time Of Awakening

You were redeemed because the Lord wants you to live in the blessings of Abraham. They are yours if you are a born-again believer in Jesus Christ and receive them through faith and by the working of the Holy Spirit in you.

The next time you take part in the bread and the cup at the Lord's table, remind yourself that you are a partaker of the covenants and their promises. Appropriate the blessings by faith when you eat the bread and drink from the cup. They are both Holy and Sacred, and your fellowship with the Lord will be intimate and personal.

Communion Encounters

Chapter 9

Follow The Blood Trail

The spiritual journey of following the blood trail from Genesis to Revelation is evident in Scripture. We have delved into this throughout the book, including the altars, Passover, and an overview of the covenants and how the blood was applied. This journey allows us to fully comprehend the impact of what Jesus has done for us and to enrich our experience of Holy Communion.

As the Lamb of God, Jesus first shed His blood in prayer before His arrest. As we follow Jesus's path, we will go beyond Calvary to see what He did with His blood as the High Priest of the New Covenant. The profound understanding and constant reminder of the totality of the blood trail will lead us to a new and inspiring place in our experience of drinking the cup of Communion.

The following verses establish a clear trail of blood for us to follow. However, it is not the blood trail but where it leads us that is most important for a more excellent Communion experience.

In The Garden

He prayed even more passionately like one

being sacrificed, until He was in such intense agony of spirit that his sweat became drops of blood, dripping onto the ground. - Luke 22:44 The Passion Translation (TPT)

This is the first place Jesus shed His blood, and the agony and intensity of His prayer are beyond our comprehension. He was bleeding so much that it dripped to the ground.

When I think of this, I am reminded of how Noah shed the blood of innocent life, and its blood baptized the earth, leading God to institute a New Covenant with Noah that is still in effect today.

It also reminds me of what God said to Cain. *What have you done? The voice of your brother's blood cries out to Me from the ground."* (Genesis 4:10) I believe the Heavenly Father knew that Jesus' innocent blood was crying out from the ground. His blood cried, Holy!It's worth noting that both parents contribute to a child's blood type.

In the case of Jesus, His blood type was a combination of Mary's and the Heavenly Father's, a holy and unique blend. This unique blend, as the following verse reminds us, underscores His divine lineage and His rightful title as the Son of God, reinforcing the significance of His blood in our faith.

And the angel answered and said to her, "The Holy Spirit will come upon you, and the power of the Highest will overshadow you; therefore, also, that Holy One who is to be born will be called the Son of God. - Luke 1:35 NKJV

"... This is why the child born to you will be holy, and he will be called the Son of God." - Luke 1:35 The Passion Translation (TPT)

Jesus Christ is Holy! He was born without sin in His bloodline, for His Father was Almighty God. That is how He could become the perfect, spotless lamb of God, who would take away the sin of the world and remove the power of sin and its penalty from us. His blood was pure and holy, just like His Father.

After His Arrest

They brought Jesus before the Sanhedrin with the high priest and others to bear false witness against Him, and the cruelty began with beatings, and the blood trail was being established.

Then some began to spit on him, and to blindfold Him, and to beat Him, and to say to Him, "Prophesy!" And the officers struck Him with the palms of their hands. - Mark 14:65 The Pasion Translation (TPT)

Communion Encounters

They Plucked Out His Beard

> *I gave my back to those who plucked out the beard, I did not hide My face from shame and spitting.* - Isaiah 50:6 NKJV

Having His beard pulled out would have been extremely painful, and He would have been dripping blood down his face and chest to the ground. The cruelty and bleeding continued.

He Was Brutally Scourged

> *Then he released Barabbas to them, and when he had scourged Jesus, he delivered Him to be crucified.* - Matthew 27:26 NKJV

When a victim was to be scourged, they would be stripped and tied to a whipping post. Then, they would beat the person without mercy with a whip consisting of several long leather thongs, each loaded with jagged pieces of metal or bone and weighted with lead on the end. Fragments of flesh would be torn from the victim, and many people did not survive the beating.

The leather strips would be long and not just go across the back, but they would cross the arms and wrap around the body to the chest, face, and legs.

A Time Of Awakening

They could bleed to death during the beating.

Crown of Thorns Then Struck In The Head

> *When they had twisted a crown of thorns,*
> *they put it on His head and a reed in His right*
> *hand. And they bowed the knee before Him*
> *and mocked Him, saying, "Hail, King of the*
> *Jews!" 30 Then they spat on Him and took the*
> *reed and struck Him on the head.* - Matthew
> 27:29-30 NKJV

The crown of thorns would be bad enough, and the
bleeding would be significant. However, they went
further and took a reed to beat the thorns deeper into
his head. He would leave a blood trail all the way to
Calvary.

They Crucify Him

> *31 And when they had mocked Him, they took*
> *the robe off Him, put His own clothes on*
> *Him, and led Him away to be crucified.* -
> Matthew 27:31 NKJV

His blood was dripping from His body on the way to
Calvary, the ultimate place of cruelty. With the nails
beaten into His hands and feet, the bleeding
continued. Like the blood of Abel crying out from
the ground, I think the blood of Jesus did as well.

Pierced After Death

> *But one of the soldiers pierced His side with a spear, and immediately blood and water came out.* - John 19:34 NKJV

After Jesus had died, Joseph and Nicodemus took His body. Per Jewish custom for burial, they bound His body in strips of linen and spices and laid Jesus in the tomb. John 20 tells a beautiful story of our Lord's resurrection and the very revealing interaction between Jesus and Mary Magdalene. But the blood trail has not ended.

I Have Not Yet Ascended

Mary was filled with overwhelming grief as she sought to find out where the Lord's body had been moved. Feeling distraught, she was unaware it was Jesus speaking with her until He said her name, Mary. She had heard Him say her name before!

> *Now when she had said this, she turned around and saw Jesus standing there, and did not know that it was Jesus.* [15] *Jesus said to her, "Woman, why are you weeping? Whom are you seeking?"*
>
> *She, supposing Him to be the gardener, said to Him, "Sir, if You have carried Him away,*

tell me where You have laid Him, and I will take Him away." 16 Jesus said to her, "Mary! She turned and said to Him, "Rabboni!"

17 Jesus said to her, "Do not cling to Me, for I have not yet ascended to My Father; but go to My brethren and say to them, 'I am ascending to My Father and your Father and to My God and your God.'" - John 20:14-17 NKJV

From the garden to the tomb, Jesus left a trail of His blood, but the trail did not end there.

Most people know Jesus ascended into heaven after giving the Great Commission, but that is the second ascension, according to Scripture.

Shortly after His resurrection, Jesus told Mary not to cling to Him because He was ascending to His Father and hers. He needed to do something else before they could touch Him, requiring Him to ascend to Heaven. This is Jesus's first ascension to heaven, and He went with His blood.

He was ascending to heaven as the High Priest after the order of Melchizedek to have an extraordinary meeting with His Father.

He told her to tell the others what He was doing, and

later that evening, He appeared to all of them.

The Perfected High Priest

As the suffering Redeemer, Jesus perfectly accomplished the Father's will, qualifying Him as the author of eternal salvation. Having been perfected, God also called Jesus to be the High Priest of the New Covenant according to the order of Melchizedek. Jesus began to function as the High Priest and entered the Most Holy Place in Heaven, which was no minor event.

> *And having been perfected, He became the author of eternal salvation to all who obey Him,* [10] *called by God as High Priest "according to the order of Melchizedek," -* Hebrews 5:9-10 NKJV

He Went Behind The Veil

When Jesus went into heaven, He entered the Presence of God behind a veil. This mirrored the actions of the earthly High Priest, who entered the Holy of Holies behind the veil in the temple to make the annual sin offering for the people's sins. Inside, he sprinkled blood on himself and throughout the Holy of Holies, including the Ark of the Covenant and the Mercy Seat. This is where God's Glory and Presence would come and reside.

When Jesus died, God tore the veil of the earthly Holy Place in two. That temple and the related functions of the earthly priesthood were over.

Now we see the High Priest of the New Covenant, who shed His blood, walking behind the veil into God's presence in heaven. He had earned the right to be the High Priest according to the order of Melchizedek. He was our forerunner, and He would open the door for us.

> *We have this hope as an anchor of the soul, both sure and steadfast, and which enters the Presence behind the veil* [20] *where the forerunner has entered for us, even Jesus, having become High Priest forever according to the order of Melchizedek.* - Hebrews 6:19-20 NKJV

He Entered With His Blood

The blood trail ends in the Holy of Holies in heaven and in the presence of God.

Jesus was the High Priest of *good things to come*, with a perfect tabernacle not made by hands.

Unlike the earthly High Priest, He would not use the blood of animals for a sin covering. With the New Covenant, Jesus, with His blood, entered the *Most*

Holy Place and walked into the presence of God for us.

He only had to do it once, and He obtained eternal redemption once for all people.

> *But Christ came as High Priest of the good things to come, with the greater and more perfect tabernacle not made with hands, that is, not of this creation. [12] Not with the blood of goats and calves, **but with His own blood He entered the Most Holy Place** once for all, having obtained eternal redemption.* - Hebrews 9:11-12 NKJV

The Passion Translation (TPT) gives an excellent description of this.

> *And He has entered once and forever into the Holiest Sanctuary of All, not with the blood of animal sacrifices, but the **sacred blood of His own sacrifice**. And He alone has made our salvation secure forever.* - Hebrews 9:12 (TPT)

He Entered God's Presence For Us

As our High Priest, Jesus appeared in God's presence on our behalf and presented His blood in the Most Holy Place in creation.

*For Christ has not entered the holy places made with hands, which are copies of the true, but into heaven itself, **now to appear in the presence of God for us**; [25] not that He should offer Himself often, as the high priest enters the Most Holy Place every year with blood of another.* - Hebrews 9:24-25 NKJV

His Conscience Changing Blood

The following Scriptures make it clear that the blood of Jesus has cleansed our consciousness of sins, which is a wonderful thought. Our hearts have been sprinkled with the blood of Jesus, so we no longer have an evil conscience.

According to II Corinthians 5:21, our consciousness of sin has been replaced with a righteousness consciousness. But you wouldn't know it by watching people take Communion in church.

During Communion, it is natural for us to remember that we were once lost in sin and how Jesus suffered and gave His life so we could receive eternal life. However, we should not linger in our thoughts at the foot of the cross.

Instead, we should focus on His resurrection, His ascension to heaven, and His soon return. He is not dead - He is alive! By remembering the whole story during Communion, we will experience more of His power, presence, and joy.

Acknowledging Jesus's work as our High Priest should shift our focus away from the sin consciousness of our old man to the righteousness consciousness, we now have in Him after being born again. Scripture tells us to put off the old man and put on the new man. Let the fullness of these meditations take you to the Holy of Holies in the presence of the Father and the High Priest of the new covenant in His blood!

> *How much more shall the blood of Christ, who through the eternal Spirit offered Himself without spot to God, **cleanse your conscience** from dead works to serve the living God?* - Hebrews 9:14 NKJV

> *For then, would they not have ceased to be offered? For the worshipers, **once purified, would have had no more consciousness of sins**.* - Hebrews 10:2 NKJV

> *Let us draw near with a true heart in full assurance of faith, having **our hearts sprinkled from an evil conscience** and our bodies washed with pure water.* - Hebrews 10:22 NKJV

A Time Of Awakening

For He made Him who knew no sin to be sin for us, that we might become the righteousness of God in Him. - II Corinthians 5:21 NKJV

Church leaders overseeing Communion in the services must lead people further down this path. The congregations are told to remember His sufferings and the price He paid for us, and we should. But that is where almost all Communion Services end, remembering His death. This is a place calling for reformation.

Leaders must take the time to lead the church into His joyful presence in Communion, which should end as a celebration of praise, as it did at Passover.

This book discusses various ways to experience Communion's benefits more fully. Leaders must move past the ritual and guide their congregations to experience Communion more fully, which takes more than just 6 minutes, pastors.

He Sat Down

When Jesus arrived in heaven, the Father welcomed Him back and then made one of the most amazing declarations in the Bible in Hebrews 1:8-9. God said to God, *"Your throne, O God, is forever and ever."* Jesus had returned to His glory!

Psalm 24:7 tells us about His arrival in heaven. After the Father made this declaration and Jesus presented Himself and His blood to the Father, God showed Him His throne, and Jesus sat down. His work was complete, and He took His rightful place at the right hand of God.

> *"Lift up your heads, O you gates! And be lifted up you everlasting doors! And the King of Glory shall come in."But to the Son, He says: "Your throne, O God, is forever and ever; A scepter of righteousness is the scepter of Your kingdom. [9] You have loved righteousness and hated lawlessness; Therefore God, Your God, has anointed You with the oil of gladness more than Your companions."* - Hebrews 1:8-9 NKJV

> *But this Man, after He had offered one sacrifice for sins forever, **sat down** at the right hand of God.* - Hebrews 10:12 NKJV

> *Looking unto Jesus, the author and finisher of our faith, who for the joy that was set before Him endured the cross, despising the shame, and has **sat down** at the right hand of the throne of God.* - Hebrews 12:2 NKJV

> *Who being the brightness of His glory and the express image of His person*

*and upholding all things by the word of His power, when He had by Himself purged our sins, **sat down** at the right hand of the Majesty on high, [4] having become so much better than the angels, as He has by inheritance obtained a more excellent name than they.* - Hebrews 1:3-4 NKJV

We Have Access To The Holiest Place

When you have Communion, think about Jesus entering His glory and sitting on His throne next to the Father.

Then, remember you have full access to the Father and Jesus by His blood.

Therefore, brethren, having boldness to enter the Holiest by the blood of Jesus, [20] by a new and living way which He consecrated for us, through the veil, that is, His flesh, [21] and having a High Priest over the house of God, [22] let us draw near with a true heart in full assurance of faith, having our hearts sprinkled from an evil conscience and our bodies washed with pure water. - Hebrews 10:19-22 NKJV

By His blood, you can come boldly into the Holy of Holies in heaven. You can walk past the veil and draw near to Him, fully aware of your right standing in Him, and know that He welcomes you at the end of the blood trail.

Chapter 10

Appropriate The Blood

In the same manner, He also took the cup after supper, saying, "This cup is the new covenant in My blood. This do, as often as you drink it, in remembrance of Me." - I Corinthians 11:25 NKJV

Communion delivers all of the blessings and promises found in the New Covenant. Whatever you need is found and can be appropriated *in Communion*. All that is within the New Covenant is found in His blood.

So, what can we find in the New Covenant that we can appropriate and receive through the Cup of the New Covenant IN His blood?

One morning, I was meditating on Jesus's words, *"This cup is the new covenant in My blood."* The Holy Spirit brought my attention to the word "in," and then He asked me, *"What is "IN" communion?"* The New Covenant is in His blood. What's in the New Covenant?

Immediately, He revealed to me that we can appropriate when we partake in Communion. His body and blood permeate every aspect of our lives and existence. Nothing is overlooked, and He withholds nothing from us. There is immense power in Communion.

I began to write down everything He imparted to me. The following is not an exhaustive list, but it includes what I received from Him, and I encourage you to contribute more to it.

What's In Communion

In Communion there is worship, giving thanks, embracing Jesus, declaration, appropriation, relationship, acknowledgment, resting in His presence, place of peace, restoration, freedom, encountering Him in greater spiritual depths, joy, celebration, anticipation, life, healing, a time of listening, a time of revelation, a place of birthing, a place of victory in spiritual warfare, remembrance, refreshing, a place of divine intimacy, holiness, redemption, justification, sanctification, cleansing, access, boldness, authority, power, blessings, provision, binding and loosing, sacredness, Holiness, fellowship with the Trinity, place of prayer, love, place of forgiveness, a place of deliverance, a place of affirmation, a place of acceptance, a place of encouragement, uplifting, renewal, a place of His presence and glory, awakening, revival, strengthening, protection, rejoicing, growth, a place of guidance, a place to hear, wisdom, understanding, knowledge, a place to see, discernment, light, heavenly citizenship, and I am sure much more.

How Do We Appropriate

For years, I have heard the term "plead the blood" and found it somewhat disheartening. Something did not resonate with me, and I discovered why in recent years. To plead made it sound like we were begging God to do something, and it sounded like hope without faith or authority.

It made me think of a person who pleads innocent or guilty in a court of law. If they plead innocent to a charge against them, they must present their case and hope the judge rules in their favor. In that example, pleading carries no weight or influence, and when applied to the blood of Jesus, it cheapens the power of His blood.

I asked the Lord to help me with this, and that is why you see me writing so much about "appropriating" or "applying" the blood.

When we "appropriate" the blood, we already know its power and the guaranteed result coming as we act in faith on the word of God within the New Covenant in His blood. Our position in Him is secure, and the results are predetermined.

When we declare our faith in Communion, we appropriate God's promises and blessings through the blood of Jesus.

Your victory is in the blood of Jesus and by the word of your testimony. That is your appropriation, and it has nothing to do with pleading, hoping, and begging.

> *And they overcame him by the blood of the Lamb and by the word of their testimony and they did not love their lives to the death.* - Revelation 12:11 NKJV

If you need peace, have Communion, and appropriate the peace of Jesus that He has already declared is yours. Finding the Bible verses that apply to your needs or desires is essential. While having Communion, apply the power of the blood of Jesus and make your proclamation. There are some great examples of this in the chapter regarding the Cups Of Communion.

Communion – The Highest Form of Spiritual Warfare

The enemies of darkness have no answer for the blood of Jesus. In delivering Israel from bondage in Egypt, the Lord declared, *"I am the Lord,"* and then He destroyed the powers of darkness and delivered

His people by applying the blood as a covering over each house. It is no different for you. You are cleansed by the blood, kept by the blood, and protected by the blood. The blood has been applied to your life Christian! Engage it in Communion.

When appropriated in faith during Communion, the blood destroys the works of the devil. The body and blood of Jesus are weapons for us to use against all principalities, powers, and rulers of darkness and must be declared in faith. Communion becomes an open exhibit of total power and authority over evil, which becomes a proclamation and statement of faith against all powers of darkness. We overcome, by the blood and the words of our proclamation.

An old hymn still sung today is *There Is Power In The Blood*, written by Lewis E. Jones. *There is power, power, wonder-working power, in the blood of the lamb. There is power, power, wonder-working power in the precious blood of the lamb."*

Process For Personal Communion

I encourage everyone to have personal Communion throughout the week. Make it a part of your personal devotions in prayer. Over time, the Holy Spirit taught me various aspects of engaging and approaching the Lord more effectively in Communion.

Communion Encounters

At a minimum, I will spend twenty to thirty minutes in Communion. When incorporated into my prayer time, it is more intense and can become several hours. In those times, I may have Communion multiple times as I pray and appropriate the blood into various situations or for others in need.

When preparing for Communion, I always have my Bible, prayer journal, and pen. I prepare a larger glass of juice and a larger piece of Matzah bread, knowing I will probably have Communion more than once, and then go to my study and close the door. It's time to meet with Jesus.

I rarely think about how long I have available because, on many days, I start this at 4:30 or 5 a.m., and I don't care how long I am there as I am meeting with Jesus. On some days, I have Communion multiple times. There is no right or wrong time, and how often is up to you.

The Lord's Prayer. I rarely get past "Our Father" because I get so focused on the fact that I get to call the Great I AM and Almighty God my Father. This always moves me to express my gratitude and thanksgiving to Him. The Holy Spirit often quickens certain Scriptures that I read and declare to Him.

As I acknowledge Who He is, I find myself moving into praise and worship. That includes declaring His

A Time Of Awakening

Holiness and calling the Angels to join me. That's when His presence becomes very strong, and His glory surrounds me. This takes time, so don't be in a hurry. Enjoy it.

I let Him know I have come to seek His presence, His face, and His glory. I will quote various verses with an attitude of prayer and a humble heart. He is God, and I am man.

I lay myself open before Him and ask Him if there is any sin I must be aware of so I can repent. I want nothing in my heart that negatively impacts or interrupts the intimacy I desire with Him. I also ask Him to show me anything in my life that offends Him and for the same reason. Then I listen.

At this point, things can go in many directions depending on the Lord's leading. Sometimes, I need to pray about things on a personal or ministry level for the churches and their leaders or our country. There is a long list of things and people to pray for.

I will always seek the Holy Spirit's guidance on what I should appropriate the body and the blood for. It is a time of spiritual warfare from a place of victory.

It seems that this time with Him does not end. Although I usually listen to worship music, I have begun celebrating Him with joyful music and thanksgiving as I leave my study and go about my day. I seem to smile more these days.

Process In Church Services Communion

It is challenging to go through the same process during a church service because this process cannot be pushed into a few minutes. However, I believe that more time should be devoted to Communion in our church services, allowing believers to fully embrace the significance of Jesus beyond the cross and celebrate Him as the Risen Lord!

In the many churches I have visited over the years, worship typically lasts for 45 minutes to an hour, with some dedicating up to two hours. While we all come together to praise and worship Jesus, I have noticed that in most churches, Communion is rushed and lasts for less than 10 minutes, which doesn't allow people to fully experience its significance. There is much more that people can glean from the Communion experience. I believe God is urging us to reform this aspect of our church services and reconsider our approach to Communion.

What would the church experience if Communion were integrated into the worship service and the leaders guided the congregation from the Cross to the Lord, sitting down in Glory with integrated teaching, altar calls, and prayer?

Imagine intertwining praise and worship with various teachings about Holy Communion and receiving Communions, along with a variety of altar calls, declarations, and prayers for a variety of needs. Then, returning to a time of praise, celebration, and testimonies.

I've seen this in several Communion Encounter services, and it's fascinating. The impact on people is truly amazing as they are being born again, recommitting their lives to Jesus, receiving emotional and physical healings and miracles, and just experiencing His presence in wonderful and overwhelming ways. Churches are changing how they approach Communion in their services based on what they have learned and experienced in our meetings.

Examine Yourself

There is a seriousness of Communion that we cannot ignore. Communion is an ordinance of the church and not a ritual. Through the blood of Jesus, we are cleansed of our sins and brought into this marvelous celebration. It is His provision, and we are invited to enjoy it with respect.

> *Therefore, whoever eats this bread or drinks this cup of the Lord in an unworthy manner will be guilty of the body and blood*

of the Lord. [28] But let a man examine himself, and so let him eat of the bread and drink of the cup. [29] For he who eats and drinks in an unworthy manner eats and drinks judgment to himself, not discerning the Lord's body.

[30] For this reason many are weak and sick among you, and many sleep. [31] For if we would judge ourselves, we would not be judged. - I Corinthians 11:27-31 NKJV

Close self-examination is important when receiving Communion. We should remember what the bread and cup represent and approach them with humility and reverence.

This passage cautions against empty participation and treating Communion as a religious ritual. Handling the bread and cup should be done respectfully, remembering they represent the Lord's body and blood. Those who partake in an unworthy manner find themselves being judged by God, and the results are described in verse 30. *"Many are weak and sick among you, and many sleep (have died)."*

Careful self-examination will help us avoid the chastisement of the Lord and even premature death.

This verse is a warning against meaningless participation in Communion. Come to the table with worship and humility and be strengthened by the Lord in joy and celebration.

> *I will take up the cup of salvation and call upon the name of the Lord.* - Psalm 116:13 NKJV

> *You prepare a table before me in the presence of my enemies. You anoint my head with oil: My cup runs over.* - Psalm 23:5 NKJV

Selah!

Communion Encounters

From The Author

About Jay Brinegar

Jay Brinegar was Ordained in January of 1982. With a ministry spanning over 45 years, he has been deeply involved in pastoral, evangelistic, prison, and street ministry. His journey has taken him across the country, where he has passionately preached the Word of God in local churches and led crusades in collaboration with numerous area churches and denominations. His ministry has also extended to foreign mission work in Haiti and Brazil, South America.

Jay's visionary leadership was instrumental in the success of Love March '88, a significant ecumenical event in Indianapolis. This event, which he spearheaded, brought together over 4,000 people from various denominations, united in their devotion to Jesus and their prayers for revival. The impact of this revival was far-reaching, extending to cities throughout Indiana and Michigan.

For three years, Jay and his wife, Patti, were instrumental in the success of a weekly television program called Street Life that aired on Dr. Lester Sumrall's LeSea Broadcasting network in Indianapolis, Indiana. Along with their television program, Patti and Jay hosted Trinity Broadcasting Networks Live "Praise The Lord" program, which aired on WCLJ-TV in Greenwood, Indiana.

Along with his pastoral ministry, Jay taught at the Indianapolis-based extension of Dr. Sumrall's World Harvest Bible College in South Bend, Indiana. He also served in multiple capacities in Full Gospel Businessmen. He was on the founding Board of Directors of Area Christian Television, responsible for establishing WCLJ-TV in Greenwood, Indiana, later owned and operated by Trinity Broadcasting Network.

As a student of revival history, Jay is an itinerant minister, speaking in conferences, churches and small gatherings with an emphasis on corporate prayer and Holy Communion to help bring awakening to the church and their communities.

Jay carries the vision of Communion Encounter services and events and has seen great manifestations of God's power and presence in these services.

For more information, to schedule him, or plan a Communion Encounter event, please email info@powerupministries.net or to learn more you can visit powerupministries.net.

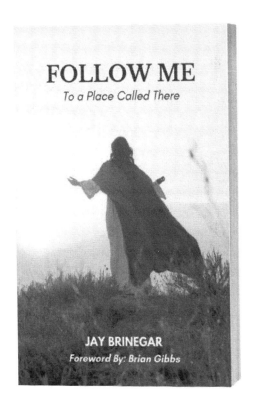

A Time Of Awakening

Jay's book, *"Follow Me To A Place Called There,"* is also available on Amazon.com and wherever books are sold.

Communion Encounters

Made in the USA
Columbia, SC
02 October 2024

42808920R00091